I0137562

WHITE SKIN, DARK SKIN, POWER, DREAM

COLLECTED ESSAYS ON LITERATURE AND CULTURE

by

Francis Jarman
University of Hildesheim

THE BORGO PRESS
An Imprint of Wildside Press
Holicong, Pennsylvania

MMV

*I.O. Evans Studies in the Philosophy
and Criticism of Literature*
ISSN 0271-9061
Number Twenty-Seven

Copyright © 2005 by Francis Jarman
All rights reserved. No part of this book may be
reproduced in any form without the expressed
written consent of the publisher.

Published in the United States of America by
The Borgo Press, an imprint of Wildside Press,
P.O. Box 301, Holicong, PA 18928-0301

FIRST EDITION

CONTENTS

INTRODUCTION

The essays in this book cover a wide range of literary and cultural topics: race, sex, the Second World War, detective novels, Kipling, torture, widow-burning, the "Great Indian Novel," travel writing, Alexandria, Lawrence Durrell, the Srebrenica Massacre, the Indian Mutiny, writers' motives for writing. But they do have a common denominator, which is that they are all concerned (though in different ways) with perception and communication across cultures.

They were written over a period of about ten years, but the arrangement here is thematic, not chronological. First, there are two essays about how we impose ways of seeing, or *discourses*, on "the world out there"; these are followed by two examples, both with a Japanese focus, of how to break out of this discursive straitjacket; then there is a group of three essays about India, touching on such questions as cultural relativism and culture shock; a survey of the possible responses to the Other in travel and travel writing; an essay which describes the invention of a famous literary landscape, Alexandria; and, finally, a rather personal piece of soul-searching – how did I come to write a particular play at the time and in the way that I did?

Some of the essays were presented at conferences or given as public lectures, but have not been published before; regarding the others, I would like to make grateful acknowledgement for the following:

"White Skin, Dark Skin, Power, Dream" first appeared in *Gender Studies in den Sozial- und Kulturwissenschaften*, edited by Sabine Wesely, Bielefeld: Kleine, 2000;

"From the Deserts of Belgium to the Jungles of Korea" was first published in *Thriving on Diversity*, edited by Jürgen Beneke, Bonn: Dümmler, 1998, and now published by Asgard (St. Augustin);

"J. G. Ballard: Through the Eyes of a Child" and "Useful Detectives" were small sections in a much longer work, *Writing Asia* (1998), that was published in microfiche by Tectum (Marburg), 1998, and in an abridged version as a book, *The Perception of Asia*, by Hildesheim University Press, 1998.

and "Burning Women" first appeared (under the title "Sati") in the online journal *CultureScan* (see the website, www.culturescan.de) in 2002.

I should like to express my gratitude to my editor at Wildside, Prof. Michael Burgess, and to thank Rosalind Flindt for helping with the illustrations. Where no translator is mentioned in the text or in the bibliography, the translations are by the author.

— Francis Jarman
University of Hildesheim

I.

WHITE SKIN, DARK SKIN, POWER, DREAM

INTRODUCTION

Some years ago I almost missed a long-distance flight from Europe to India. Arriving late at the airport, I discovered that the flight had been overbooked and that I had been "bumped" from my Economy Class seat; however, as luck would have it, I could still be accommodated (if I so wished) in First Class. On the long flight to India I therefore found myself sitting, in unaccustomed comfort, next to a retired Indian military man of very high rank. Fortified by gin tonics, he took great trouble to explain the world's problems to me, not hesitating to suggest solutions of his own to the crises in South Africa, Northern Ireland, the Middle East, and so on. Suddenly he broke off, in mid-sentence, with an exclamation of outrage. "How could they! It's an abomination! This is First Class!" Our stewardess was *hideous*, he declared, such a monstrosity could hardly be tolerated in the vicinity of First Class passengers. Why was she not serving the plebs in Economy (if they had to give her a job at all)? Presumably she was one of a "quota" of low-caste stewardesses that they were obliged to employ for political reasons. I looked in the direction in which he was still gesticulating, but saw only a very pretty and charming South Indian girl. Then he pointed to another stewardess, this one rather taller, lighter-skinned and somewhat plain-featured, and bellowed, "Yes! *That* is what we need here in First Class!" And then it dawned on me. He had seen only the skin colour of the two girls, and hence their *race* – the one, a wheaten-skinned Kashmiri, the other, a dark-skinned Tamil – and that for him was the sole basis for deciding whether they were beautiful.

I have chosen to begin with this personal anecdote because it is such a clear statement of the racist position: beauty, refinement or other personal qualities have no bearing, only race counts. Also, because although in the following I shall mostly be discussing *white* racism, it is important to remember that racist mechanisms exist in other cultures as well (in the West we may sometimes have taken our racial guilt and self-loathing to unnecessary extremes, forgetting that skin colour racism is not uniquely something that white men do). Nevertheless, it was the white-skinned who spread themselves as conquerors and colonists across most of the non-white-skinned world, and who made skin colour an essential part of the power systems and ideologies that they installed in the territories that they brought under their control.

It could be argued that white colonists, far from inventing these mechanisms of racial superiority, already had functioning models for exploitative relationships and the discourses that underpinned them. Such analogies could be found, for instance, in the well-established complexes of class and gender that already existed in the metropolitan centres. Gender, for example, is very obviously about role, and the structuring of power relationships, and not simply about the putative effects of biological difference on social behaviour. It would be tempting, in this context, to reverse the terms in the title of the 1972 John Lennon song *Woman is the Nigger of the World*. Yet a simple substitution of paradigms is not enough. Class and gender each had an important part to play in the colonies in its own right, and there were areas of overlapping and cross-fertilisation. Anne McClintock (1995) talks of "the dangerous crossings of class, race and gender" (p.128), and it is hard to disagree with her view that they "are not distinct realms of experience, existing in splendid isolation from each other" but that they "come into existence *in and through* relation to each other" (p.5). Indeed, nowhere is this more evident than in the colonial or imperial situation, where class, race and gender meshed and conflicted with each other both in everyday life and in ideology. Using fictional material from a number of different colonial/imperial contexts (British, French, and Russian), the present essay will concern itself with conceptions of race and gender, showing how gender was (and to a great extent still is) involved in perceptions and fantasies that governed white interaction with the non-white races.

THE COLONIAL MYSTIQUE

In Henry Rider Haggard's classic Victorian adventure novel *King Solomon's Mines* (1885), the lovely African girl Foulata willingly gives up her own life to save the European whom she worships, Captain Good (note the name!). She knows that her love for the Captain is a hopeless cause: "Say to my lord . . . that – I love him, and that I am glad to die because I know that he cannot cumber his life with such as me, for the sun cannot mate with the darkness, nor the white with the black" (p. 226 f.). And again:

> The poor creature was no ordinary native girl, but a person of great, I had almost said stately, beauty, and of considerable refinement of mind. But no amount of beauty or refinement could have made an entanglement between Good and herself a desirable occurrence, for, as she herself put it, "Can the sun mate with the darkness, or the white with the black?" (p.241).

Although it would be hard to find a more poignant example of selfless love, a serious relationship between Foulata and the Captain is out of the question – the barrier of skin colour is too high to cross.

Interracial sex was a sensitive topic in the colonial world. It was felt (no doubt rightly) that too much intimacy or camaraderie between the races could lead to a growing lack of respect for the white man. Any such erosion was dangerous, because colonial rule was at least partly based on the mystique of white superiority, a bluff by which a comparatively small number of Europeans persuaded enormous numbers of their colonial subjects that it would be best for them to do as they were told (the message was also underlined by the display of military "high tech" in occasional punitive actions). The British took this mystique to extreme lengths, secretively and snobbishly excluding the natives from their clubs and many of their rituals, and indulging in eccentric, contextually inappropriate behaviour – as the song by Noel

9

Coward (1932) puts it, "Mad dogs and Englishmen go out in the mid-day sun" (p. 7).

The image that the British projected was often one of at least superhuman competence, if not godlike wisdom. Some British colonial heroes like John Nicholson actually became the objects of fanatical religious worship – reportedly, a Hindu cult to his name still exists in the Punjab (Theon Wilkinson, 1976, p. 44). The advantages and dangers of gambling on this mystique are shown in Rudyard Kipling's short story, "The Man Who Would Be King" (1888). Two renegade adventurers from British India, Daniel Dravot and Peachey Carnehan, set out to seek their fortune in the wilds of Kafiristan. By a stroke of luck – and a case of mistaken identity – they are spectacularly successful. Just as it may have helped the conquistador Hernán Cortes, when he landed in Mexico, that he was assumed to be the Aztec god Quetzalcóatl, so Daniel and Peachey willingly allow themselves to be taken for gods or devils, and install themselves as kings. Their downfall comes when Daniel makes the mistake of demanding a native girl as a wife. In fear that the terrifying god or devil will destroy her when they mate, the girl who has been chosen to be Daniel's queen bites him, and when the native people see the blood flow they turn on Daniel and Peachey, with murderous results. There is a moral here for Kipling's fellow-countrymen in the colonies: if British men become intimate with native girls there will always be the danger of that metaphorical "bite" that makes them look ridiculous and harmless, robbing them of their power.

This is not to say that there was no interracial sex throughout the British Empire. There was a great deal of illicit, usually exploitative, sexual contact – both hetero- and homosexual – between the races, as recent work on the subject (notably Ronald Hyam, 1990) has shown. Nor is it true that interracial relationships were completely taboo throughout the colonial world. In many colonies concubinage – *nyai* in the East Indies, *congai* in Indochina, *petite épouse* in the French colonial world – was encouraged for practical reasons, to keep colonial men "physically and psychologically fit for work" (Ann Laura Stoler, 1991, p. 60). It was a plank of French colonial policy in west Africa until the twentieth

10

century, "as desirable for the health and hygiene, discipline and prestige of the French official as it was for his imperial authority and linguistic competence" (Hyam, p.157). In Sarawak, ruled by the "white Rajahs" of the Brooke family, it was felt that the presence of too many white women might prevent the young district officers from getting to know the country, and the young officers were encouraged to keep housekeeper-mistresses, sometimes known as "sleeping dictionaries" (Charles Allen, 1983, p. 151 f.).

But what was actually going on (or was not going on) between the races in the colonies need not be the sole focus of our interest. In nineteenth- and twentieth-century discursive treatments of racial Self and Other – for instance, the discourse of colonial power, and the Pacific War discourse of racial confrontation between white and yellow – the images of male-female interracial relations that were presented in books and films had powerful and sometimes surprising symbolic value.

SYMBOLIC SUBJECTION

The (non-white) native woman sexually subjected to the (white) male colonist was a graphic expression of the colonial power situation, with the racial power relationship being symbolised by the gender power relationship. For Richard Cronin, in his study of fiction about India (1989), this is the dominant metaphor of *Orientalism*: "The West is a man, the East is a woman" (p. 147).

As described by Edward Said (1978), Orientalism is the manipulative European-American discourse of the Middle East, in particular Islam; however, the term has since come to be applied, more broadly, to Western discourse(s) of Asia or, indeed, of any non-Western part of the world. I have borrowed Cronin's comment, and part of the analysis of the British literary examples that follows, from my study of the Western discourse of Asia in postwar popular literature and culture in English, which focuses particularly on the Western image of Japan (Jarman, 1998c). This also contains a detailed treatment of the "novel of desertion" – especially in the Japanese context – which for reasons of space is discussed only

11

very briefly in the following section of this present essay (see also Jarman, 1998a).

The Orientalist metaphor is blatantly sexist. The (female) non-Western world requires to be awoken to life by a (male) Western kiss; protected by the West; taught (Western) discipline; have its barren culture fertilised (by a Western seed); and to be spoken for and "explained" by its more articulate (Western) friend and interpreter. Cronin comments, slyly, "It is not hard to guess how [this metaphor] came to be selected, and why it proved so useful" (p. 148).

Although the woman/native was expected to adopt a pose of admiring submissiveness – ideally, cowering at the feet of "Sahib", "Massa" or "Bwana" and gazing up in adoration – too much passive acquiescence could be interpreted as implying that the master's rule over the slave was only on the latter's sufferance. The power relations had therefore to be defined by being *enacted*. The colonial masters must crack the whip; in the male/female relationship, the man had either to rape the woman or, more subtly, to seduce and then abandon her, if he was to make his (*i.e.*, white) superiority absolutely clear. *His* will must be enforced, *her* wishes ignored or overridden, if need be with violence.

It was Susan Brownmiller (1975) who first drew wide attention to the idea that rape was less a crime of lust than an actual but also symbolic demonstration of power. In the political dimension, rape used in this way is as old as the Greeks and Romans, and as modern as the French war in Algeria, the American war in Vietnam, the Pakistani terrorisation of their breakaway province in Bengal, and the "ethnic cleansing" in the Balkans. Let us briefly consider two representative examples, seventeen centuries apart. In his *Annales*, Tacitus describes how the British king Prasutagus of the Iceni had hoped, shortly before his death, to preserve his little kingdom and his personal household from Roman aggression by a show of submissiveness, and by making the Emperor co-heir with his daughters. But the king had been presumptuous. After his death, Roman soldiers moved in to take over the kingdom, and the Iceni were taught a graphic lesson: "Kingdom and household alike were plundered like prizes of war [...] As a beginning, [Prasutagus'] widow Boudicca was

12

flogged and their daughters raped" (p. 318). (In this case, the Roman plan backfired rather badly – Boudicca took her revenge by leading a rebellion in which thousands of Romans were massacred.)

Second example: within the British Isles, rape was used as a tactic of racial intimidation and demonstration of power in the hegemonial-colonial wars between the English and their immediate neighbours. After the battle of Culloden (1746), which ended the uprising known as the "Forty-Five", rape was one of the weapons employed to demoralise the rebellious highland clans of Scotland:

> Where the River Doe meets the Moriston in a black waterfall, Isobel Macdonald was raped by five soldiers, and her husband, skulking high in the heather, watched this in agony. There were other women raped, too, and always before the doors of their burning homes (John Prebble, 1961, p. 205).

English rape of Scottish women has since become a visible element in the nationalist discourse of "Scotland the Brave" that is presently fuelling the independence movement in Scotland – and as such figures prominently in a number of recent anti-English Hollywood films set in the Scottish past, such as *Rob Roy* (1994) and *Braveheart* (1994).

An even more effective way to break the will of colonised peoples to resist was to strip their men of their "manhood" by homosexual rape or exploitation. This was never officially condoned, but it occurred nevertheless and is also an occasional element in fictional writing about the colonial situation. The sexuality of native men was seen as a particular threat, for the following very good reason: because of the unwillingness of the Westerners to allow any human contacts between colonised and colonisers of the kind that might undermine Western prestige, sex between a white woman and a native was a powerful idea that could wreak havoc among established colonial power relationships. The symbolic value of homosexual humiliation was that it "desexed" or "castrated" non-white men, negating their masculinity and sexual attractiveness.

13

It was also an appropriate punishment for rape of a white woman, a crime with which white racists were famously obsessed – and not only in the European colonies, but also in the Southern states of America, where this obsession became a standard *topos* of Southern writing, and in other parts of the world where white and non-white races lived side by side.

Whenever a native male had anything to do with a white woman the suspicion of rape was immediately, necessarily present. It could be nothing else *but* rape, because the idea that a white woman might find a non-white male sexually attractive was totally abhorrent to most white men. E. M. Forster's *A Passage to India* (1924) is the best-known fictional treatment of this theme, but it is more substantially worked out in the four parts of Paul Scott's *Raj Quartet* (1966-75), which, unlike Forster's novel, show the colonial's sexual presumption followed not merely by arrest but also by his consequent homosexual humiliation. In the clearest possible statement of the interconnection between race and gender in the colonial situation, Scott reveals how the "rape" of a white woman, Daphne Manners, inevitably leads to the sexual and sadistic abuse of her Indian boyfriend, Hari Kumar, by a British policeman, Merrick.

The first of the novels, *The Jewel in the Crown* (1966), defines the problem. In the colonial situation there was always a "hump" which, "however hard you tried, still lay in the path of thoughts you sent flowing out to a man or woman whose skin was a different colour from your own" (p.64); there was always the "little obstacle of the colour of the skin" (p. 82). White and non-white are separated by a river (rivers and bridges are major symbols in the *Quartet*), and you "had to take your courage in your hands and enter the flood and let yourself be taken with it, lead where it may" (p. 151). Because white women, with their physical vulnerability and restricted social freedom of movement, most obviously symbolised the false racial superiority of the whites in colonial apartheid, it was white women who had the broadest river to cross and the most fearsome existential leap to be undertaken. And, as if challenged by their more difficult role in the colonial situation, the white women in Scott's

14

novels truly *are* more interesting and more enterprising than the men – women are the voice of criticism and the catalysts of movement and change.

Daphne Manners is punished terribly for transgressing the social and sexual codes of British India. She is indeed raped – though not by her boyfriend. After she has given herself freely to *one* Indian man, she then finds herself taken violently by others, who have observed that the taboo on sex with a white woman has already been broken and assume therefore that the woman is now fair game. The white community seems unable or unwilling to distinguish between these two sexual encounters. In *The Towers of Silence* (1971), Major Mackay somewhat daringly speculates that Hari Kumar and Daphne Manners may have been in love with each other rather than merely the main parties in a rape situation, but this theory is found "peculiarly unacceptable" by the other members of the British club (p. 104 f.).

The police officer, Ronald Merrick, feels a particularly strong need to establish what people's social roles should be:

> You have to draw a line. . . . This side of it is right. That side is wrong. Then you have your moral term of reference. Then you can act. You can feel committed. You can be involved. Your life takes on something like a shape. It has form. Purpose as well, maybe. You know who you are when you wake up in the morning (*The Day of the Scorpion*, 1968, p. 223 f.).

Merrick is strongly opposed to any relaxation in the rigid social relationships required by colonialism. As a socially inferior, relatively low-class outsider he tends to see these relationships existentially, as "situations", rather than as part of his imperial birthright. One consequence of this is that Merrick is able to articulate feelings that, in contrast, are merely submerged and instinctive in most of the other British characters. He makes a clear distinction between sex between a white man and an Indian woman, in which the white man "has the dominant role, whatever the colour of his partner's skin", and sex between a white woman and an Indian man:

15

"A dark-skinned man touching a white-skinned woman will always be conscious of the fact that he is – diminishing her. She would be conscious of it too" (p. 226). Merrick restores the balance by torturing and sexually humiliating the "dark-skinned man" in this case, Hari Kumar, in a "situation of enactment" (p. 306). His intention is to make both of them aware of the reality of the relationship between ruler and ruled. As Kumar explains: "[Merrick] said that if people would enact a situation they would understand its significance." The girl Daphne has less and less to do with this: "He said I could forget the girl. What had happened to her was unimportant" (p. 308). The significant relationship is the power relationship between the two men, the white and the non-white, with the need (from Merrick's point of view) to find a way of restoring the balance in favour of the former. Kumar: "It was a question of extracting everything possible from the situation while it lasted. [...] The situation of our being face to face, with everything finally in his favour" (p.291). What matters is race and power, not sexuality. The sexual domination of one man by the other is a means to an end. Afterwards, says Kumar, "He said we both knew where things stood now" (p. 310).

THE NOVEL OF DESERTION

Since Medea and Cleopatra, women from the East in particular have been associated with magic, danger and voluptuous sexuality. In the nineteenth and twentieth centuries, the spread of Western power throughout the world (with, concomitantly, greater mobility for Westerners), a hunger for the exotic combined with contempt for the non-European, and the example of sexual adventurism set by the writings of Byron, Nerval, Flaubert, Loti and many others since then, all combined to create substantial numbers of Western "sex tourists" and a still larger readership for escapist erotic fantasy. Non-European women provided an object for the projection of erotic daydreams and secret desires.

It may have been Pierre Loti (the pen-name of the French naval officer Louis Marie Julien Viaud, 1850-1923) who launched the genre of the "novel of desertion" (Earl

Miner, 1958, p. 48) with his narcissistic fictionalisation of conquests made in such exotic ports of call as Constantinople (*Aziyadé*, 1879), Tahiti (*Le Mariage de Loti*, 1880) or Nagasaki (*Madame Chrysanthème*, 1887); however, examples of this kind of writing can be found in every era in which men have travelled, in consciousness of their racial and cultural superiority, as conquerors, or colonists, or merely as arrogant tourists – and the exploitation and casting aside (or "killing off") of the native girl has been a symbolic statement of that superiority. Aeneas savouring the physical charms of the exotic Queen Dido (in Book Four of Virgil's *Aeneid*), before abandoning her when "duty calls", is perhaps the first famous example.

The British and French tales of desertion are the best-known, but there is an interesting, if less obvious, Russian story of this type tucked away inside Lermontov's novel *Geroy nashego vremeni* (1839-40, translated as *A Hero of Our Time*, 1966). Pechorin, a young Russian officer in the (colonial) Caucasus, abducts and seduces a beautiful fifteen- or sixteen-year-old Circassian girl, Bela. He wins her trust, even her love, but then gets bored with her. She makes a change from his usual aristocratic conquests, but, as he says, "a native girl's love is little better than that of a lady of rank. The ignorance and simplicity of the one are as tiresome as the coquetry of the other" (p. 53 f.). Before he can abandon her, however, she is abducted once again, this time by a Circassian admirer, and fatally wounded in the chase and mêlée that follow. Pechorin is responsible not only for the girl's death (because of his having abducted her in the first place, and because of the example that he sets for Kazbich, the Circassian admirer, to follow) but also for the death of her father and the ruin of her brother.

Pechorin's fellow officer Maxim Maximych narrates the story, but his narration is in turn embedded in the first-person narration by the author, Lermontov (or his spokesman), an interesting device which sets up a tension between the two narrative viewpoints, inviting the reader either to identify with the decent, mildly disapproving Maxim Maximych or to see him as an unreliable narrator whose criticism of Pechorin is not necessarily shared by the author. Maxim

17

Maximych is indeed not very impressed by Pechorin's plan to abduct Bela, which he thinks is a "bad business" (p. 36). And: "I told Pechorin so afterwards, but he only answered that an uncivilized Circassian girl should be glad to have a nice husband like him, since, after all, *according to their ways* he would be her husband" (my emphasis).

Here, in Pechorin's response, is the crux of the matter: he has tricked the girl into believing in him, but he takes neither her nor the relationship seriously. It is serious only by *her* standards, and the man's contempt for these is part of the generalised contempt of the West for the non-Western Other. A Madam Butterfly may think that she is married to a Pinkerton, but the Pinkerton knows that it is only a local Japanese arrangement and that it need not stand in the way of his getting a "proper wife" back home in the United States. Yet there is little point in criticising these male exploiters for being contemptuous or ironical - if, as I have suggested, the reason for the whole discursive exercise is the enactment of a racial power situation, then too much sensitivity on the part of the male protagonists, too much niceness in the portrayal of the deserted maidens, would surely defeat its whole purpose.

From within the genre, some individual works of great distinction have been created, which reflect critically on the situation and deepen our understanding of it – Pearl S. Buck's *The Hidden Flower* (1952), which displays its author's ability to identify cross-culturally and to express cultural nuances with linguistic sensitivity, is arguably one such work. The opera *Madama Butterfly* (1904), on the other hand, is not: despite the pathos of Butterfly's situation, Puccini is unwilling to show the one-sidedness and trickery in the "love" between Butterfly and Pinkerton by *musical* means, and the heartrendingly beautiful music makes it almost impossible to maintain a critical stance *vis-à-vis* what is happening on the stage.

A few years ago, the Butterfly story was brilliantly deconstructed by the Chinese-American playwright David Henry Hwang (*M. Butterfly*, 1988). Hwang tells the story of a French diplomat, Gallimard, who becomes obsessed with a beautiful Peking Opera star, Song Liling (who is actually a male actor who specialises in female roles). They become lovers, and their relationship lasts for twenty-five years, but when Song's true identity is revealed, Gallimard is disgraced and, in the final scene, changes from "Pinkerton" to "Butterfly" and kills himself in the traditional manner by *seppuku*. On the one hand, the plot device seems ridiculous and implausible, even though the play is apparently based on an authentic case of mistaken sexual identity involving a French diplomat and a Peking Opera singer, and a similar – and wholly convincing – transvestite trick is played, not only on the gullible boyfriend but also on the audience, by the British film *The Crying Game* (1992). On the other hand, the device is powerfully symbolic: Gallimard-Pinkerton is unable to see who his lover really is because he is trapped in discursive prejudices and fantasies. He is searching solipsistically for an exotic Other that is really an extension of his Self, and so the search ends where it has to end, with Gallimard *becoming* Butterfly.

CONTEMPT AND BETRAYAL

Once away from home, many Western males treated non-Western women as a sexual playground, even indulging in taboo or disturbing forms of sexual behaviour like child abuse, anal sex, sexual torture and sexual killing; at home, they could still read about such things (or, today, watch pornographic films). Some may have been motivated by a desire to escape, in reality or in imagination, the increasingly critical, self-assertive women of the West, who were beginning to challenge traditional gender structures and showing less and less enthusiasm for male hegemony – or at least they my have rationalised their behaviour in these terms. In the post-war Western world there was also, at least until the arrival of AIDS, a growing difference of mood, a feeling of sexual opportunity, especially for men, and of "anything goes".

Sex now became part of the wallpaper of exotic background colour in films and novels. As a very mild example, let us take Jean Lartéguy's novel of South-East Asia, *Enquête sur un crucifié* (1973, translated as *Presumed Dead*, 1978). This is full of dubious sexual hints. In a bar, the narrator is invited to buy a Cambodian girl "of twelve or thirteen", who has "the fragile grace of a hind, and big dark frightened eyes"; "you'll get her to do your housework and cooking," he is told, "and, when you feel like it, you'll screw her" (p. 292). He notices another man in the bar feasting his eyes on the little girl (p. 296). Then there is "a pretty Eurasian girl", "fourteen or fifteen, with long limbs, finely chiselled features, a short nose and nice little breasts" (p.311), who makes eyes at the narrator, wiggles her hips at him, finds him attractive and is reportedly "itching" for him (p. 313).

But the enthusiasm for non-European sexuality created an awkward ideological problem: If sex with native women was so good, and guilt-free, did that mean that their culture was superior to that of Westerners? One solution was to see the native population as healthy, simple and uncomplicated, in contrast to the overbred Westerners. The writer W. Somerset Maugham, for example, was delighted when an experienced American sea-captain confirmed his opinion that native girls were better in bed than white ones, "for he had already formed the theory that native women were healthy erotic animals while white women were neurotic bitches" (Ted Morgan, 1980, p. 243). In *Presumed Dead*, the narrator, after having sex with his "first Asiatic", Mitsy, observes that "not once did she indulge in those vulgar gestures which most Western women take the liberty of making after a certain degree of intimacy has been reached" and that "the sin of the flesh did not derive from the Church and its teaching but from Western women who did not know how to behave after making love" (Lartéguy, 1973, p. 279 f.).

Another solution was to dismiss the native women as being morally inferior etc. (even while they were being exploited), thereby making it easier to keep them at an emotional distance. By this interpretation, Asian women, for instance, are superficially appealing, but tend to be treacherous and false, and not really what they seem. In *Presumed Dead*, an exquisite, aloof Vietnamese girl proves to be unexpectedly amenable: "Can do fucky-fucky" (p. 171; for the less street-credible *Moyen baiser*, p. 213 in the original). Her Western boyfriend gone, another Vietnamese girl in the same novel quickly returns to her job as a nightclub singer and to

20

her "other work". "These Vietnamese girls aren't what they seem" (p. 248).

These perceptions of falseness or deceit are a characteristic obsession in French colonial fiction, where a common theme is that of *betrayal*. Unlike the British, who tended to keep their colonial subjects at arm's length and not regard them as British in any significant sense, the French were more concerned to share with their native subjects the advantages of the French language and literature, culture, and lifestyle. (Though when the emotional embrace of that civilising mission was rejected, as in Vietnam and Algeria, the French reaction was like that of an offended lover: petty and vindictive.) In their fiction of interracial intimacy both the British and the French reveal themselves to be racist and exploitative, but the French want to be loved, and react spitefully when this fails to happen, while the British often don't really seem to care.

In this respect it is interesting to compare two novels, one British, one French, set in French Vietnam: Graham Greene's *The Quiet American* (1955) and Jean Hougron's *Soleil au ventre* (1952, translated as *Blaze of the Sun*, 1954). In *The Quiet American*, Fowler's Vietnamese mistress Phuong is just a plaything, "an atttractive simpleton" who "resembles an affectionate puppy who likes to lick its master's face and to do little tricks on command" (Michael Shelden, 1994, p. 401). The real tension in the story is between the two men, the tired, cynical, opium-smoking Briton Fowler, who will do anything in order not to become "involved" (p.27), and the naive, rather obnoxious American idealist Pyle (whose name, with its associations of haemorrhoids, reflects Greene's deep-seated anti-Americanism). Fowler's relationship with his mistress is low-key – "I want her around, I want her in my bed" (p. 132). Pyle, the much younger man, takes Phuong away from him by promising her love and marriage, and Fowler is stung into vengeful action, but only very slowly, and only after he has rationalised his motivation in political terms – Pyle has been aiding and abetting dangerous terrorists – rather than solely personal ones. He gets Phuong back in the end, but the whole business has really been something between the two men, and Fowler is haunted by the idea of wanting to say "sorry" (p. 189).

Unlike Fowler, Hougron's central figure in *Blaze of the Sun*, Lastin, is very highly sexed. When he meets the Vietnamese girl My-Diem for the first time, he notices the "heavy animal glance" (p. 9) that she gives him, "that suave glance which had taken in his body when he passed her" (p.12). Despite all the evidence that she is loyal to her pathetic husband Ronsac (who once saved her life), Lastin becomes obsessed with her, mad with the idea that she is not a "paragon of domestic virtues", but "something quite different" (p. 50). He notices the "greedy way she [has] of moistening her lips with the tip of her tongue", and declares that she is "made for joy – not exactly joy but pleasure" (p.66). She buys her own and her husband's way out of Vietminh captivity by selling her body to the Vietminh commandant (apparently enjoying it), and she almost causes the death of Lastin after her escape. When he meets her again in Saigon and dances with her, he feels her "soft flesh beneath his fingers" and thinks: "she's a dirty little slut" (p. 148; in the original French, *une sale petite garce*, p. 198) who has lied to him and tried to kill him. Although – or perhaps because? – he still sees her as a "slut" (p. 160, 176) he seduces her. Lastin tries everything that he can to wean her away from her husband, but he is frustrated by "her absurd fidelity to her given word" and by "what she persisted in calling betrayal" (p. 235). Even when he persuades her to go away with him, she abandons him to return to her dying husband. The ending of the story is left open, with My-Diem telling him to go away and Lastin sure that she will return to him "one day" (p.340).

My-Diem and Phuong are native mistresses/wives, and as such are assumed to be cheap and potentially sexually available (assumptions that would not be made so quickly in connection with a white wife or mistress). Lastin can only win My-Diem by persuading her to be treacherous, yet the more she responds to him sexually, the more preoccupied he becomes with sluttishness, betrayal and disloyalty. His own behaviour in undermining Ronsac's marriage seems contemptible, but does that mean that Lastin is intended to be an unreliable focaliser? Perhaps we find it harder today to identify with lustful passion than French readers of fifty years ago did. Lastin is trapped in a confused colonial nexus in which a white man is expected to lust for a non-white woman but cannot respect her, while she will earn his contempt ("slut") if she responds to his passion. In fact, both the main characters are wrestling unsuccessfully with stereotypes of how white men and non-white women are supposed to relate to each other in a colonial context.

Without forgetting the real opportunities for sexual exploitation or sexual escapism that these contacts provided, our concern so far has been mostly with the *signification* of relations between white men and non-white women within Western discourses of racial alterity, with gender as a means of symbolising, even enacting, the power relationships between the races. But in addition to this mechanism, there are a number of other factors to be considered, however, which derive essentially from a *reversal* or *variation* of the standard image of the white (man) lording it over the non-white (woman).

ENERGISING MYTHS

One of the commonest illustrations on the covers of stories or comics about the Second World War in the Pacific is that of the white prisoner cowering at the feet of a triumphant Japanese – perhaps a British, American or Australian POW waiting to be decapitated. Here is a spectacular and (to many Westerners) shocking reversal of the traditional colonial/imperial relationship between the races.

The purpose of publishing and circulating these images (at least during the war years and, one might argue, for only very slightly different reasons for many years afterwards) was not simply documentation of war-crimes or of racial humiliation – it was to shock Westerners into becoming indignant, and fiercely anti-Japanese.

These are images with which emotional energy can be released; the stories behind them are "energising myths" to make men angry and make them want to fight and kill. I have borrowed the term "energising myth" from Martin Green (1979, p. 3), who uses it in the more positive context of adventure stories that inspired people to want to go out and join the colonial/imperial adventure, but the principle is the same, and how much more effective these energising myths would be if the non-white male were shown sexually humiliating the white man, in a direct reversal of the common pattern!

This can happen in several ways. First, there is direct physical, usually anal, assault on a helpless white prisoner. This is threatened, for instance, in Klaus Netzen's *Pearl of Blood* (1975), and actually carried out (in the form of the water torture) in Eric Lambert's *The Dark Backward* (1958), in which the narrator is shown the "violated body" (p. 55) of his comrade Jack:

> Jack lay on the floor on his belly. He was naked. Two Japs stood over him. A length of hose ran out from between his legs into a bucket of water wherein a stirrup pump stood. A Jap was pumping at it but ceased when I stumbled in... They all ceased. (p. 52).

Although this is the water torture, and not sodomy, the language ("violated body", "naked") and imagery (the length of hose between Jack's legs, the Japanese "pumping") is sexually suggestive. Other novels, like Christopher Nicole's *Lord of the Golden Fan* (1973) and *The Sun Rises* (1984), contain explicit scenes in which the European hero is sexually humiliated and anally raped by Japanese.

A more common device is to show the rape or sexual abuse of white women, if possible with white men being forced to stand by impotently and watch as the conquerors "take" "their" women. As I suggested above, it has to be rape – the possibility of white women *willingly* going with non-white men is something that many white men are completely unable to accept. This is a very common theme in colonial and Pacific War writing. In one of the semi-pornographic "classics" of women's POW camp fiction, *The Camp on Blood Island* (1958), which harps on the sexual abuse of women prisoners and even contains a "slave market" scene of women being inspected and fondled by the Japanese commandant, the white prisoners are raped or compelled to sleep with the Japanese, and only the *half-caste* Mala goes with them willingly, in return for chocolate and condensed milk.

Ann Laura Stoler (1991) has noted the seeming paradox that non-white men were assumed to lust after white women who were only of limited sexual interest to white men themselves: "Although [...] in novels and memoirs European women were categorically absent from the sexual fantasies of colonial men, the very same men deemed them to be desired and seductive figures to men of color" (p. 67). Stoler's assertion about the sexual daydreams of the white colonial masters is not completely true – for example, illicit sex with the wives of British fellow officers plays an important role in the pornographic novel *Venus in India* (1889), by Captain Charles Devereaux – but in British India flirtations (and, occasionally, adulterous sex) with married white women and the sexual exploitation of Indian women were activities that occurred in two completely different dimensions, with Eurasian (in modern terminology, Anglo-Indian) women forming an interesting "in-between" case.

The Japanese actually showed, under horribly inviting circumstances, comparatively little interest in raping white women, unless ordered to do so as part of an "ethnic cleansing"-type terror campaign (as happened during the siege and fall of Hong Kong, for example); they much preferred Chinese or other Asian women, and tended to find Europeans too large, clumsy, loud, hairy and smelly for their taste. And although there was a European panic and hysteria about rape during the Indian Mutiny (1857-58), scarcely any white women actually seem to have been sexually abused. (I have examined and speculated about the fate of the two best-known "cases", Ulrica Wheeler and Amy Horne, in my stage-play *A Star Fell*, 1998b.)

There are several reasons to be found for this obsession with the rape of white women by non-whites. One is that it is, as already suggested, a means – an "energising myth" – to outrage white males, not because of what actually happens to the unfortunate woman, but because of the symbolic challenge to their own dignity and status. The rapist is seen as being not so much sexually obsessed with his victim – white men are not at ease with the idea that non-white men could quite legitimately be fascinated by the white, female Other – as trying to hurt, undermine and destroy white male power. In Tom Clancy's *Debt of Honour* (1994), Japanese gloat over the sexual exploitation of blonde American women. The villain, Goto, says, "I love fucking Americans" (p. 209), and another Japanese says that "fucking Americans will soon be our national sport" (p. 435). But this is metaphor as well as straightforward erotic aggressiveness. Goto and his friend will get their kicks not from the American women, but from doing it to them in front of American men, and the way they talk is not so far away from the kind of thing that businessmen mean when they use such sexual metaphors as "screwing" (disadvantaging) or "shafting" (defeating) the opposition. And, besides, there is a strategy of forward causality at work here – the outraging of a white woman by a non-white man overturns the established structures that govern dealings between the races, thereby provoking and justifying the savage revenge that usually follows.

There is a good example of this in *The Camp on Blood Island*. Colonel Lambert, the hero, spies on the evil Colonel Yamamitsu and sees him humiliate the white girl Evaline; this is immediately followed by Lambert taking excessively brutal revenge on the Japanese. What has Yamamitsu done to deserve this? Although he is obviously enjoying Evaline's favours, all that Lambert actually sees is the white girl kneeling to wash the yellow man's hair, and then Yamamitsu striking her once with a riding crop. The beating that Lambert gives him is far, far worse. What particularly outrages Lambert is when the Japanese refers to Evaline as *his* woman ("You can have my woman, Lambert. She very good –", p. 116): "Lambert hit him once more with the riding crop. 'I don't like white women to be talked of like that when there is yellow trash present,' he said, softly." Here, as in other, similar, fictional texts, the act of revenge is itself a demonstrative re-establishment of the proper racial order of things.

There are other possible reasons for the rape obsession, including some that may have to do with sexual masochism or latent homosexuality. Alternatively, taboo fantasies are projected onto the exotic racial Other, who acts them out

26

as proxy for the fantasist (here, it is African men in particular who are the preferred inflictors of sexual outrage on helpless white women, perhaps because of the white male preoccupation with such matters as the size of the black penis).

GENDER ACROSS CULTURES

Women are also allowed to dream, in this case of an exotic Other who is more romantic, more sensitive, more sexually adept, better hung, or simply more interesting than the men they grew up with and are used to. This is the world of *The Sheik* and of Mills & Boon publications, and of being initiated into sexual delights by (to take a few examples from popular fiction) a highly-sexed Chinese mandarin in *The English Concubine* (Jonathan Quayne, 1968), an Indian prince in *A Rose in the Banyan Tree* (1979) or a "mysterious Eurasian tycoon" in *Love in the China Sea* (Judith Baker, 1983).

In my discussion of the *Raj Quartet,* I pointed out how much more interesting the women in these novels were than the men, and that it was they who were the catalysts of movement and change. Potentially, women have a considerable advantage over men in situations of cross-cultural interaction, in that they are often more intuitive and emotionally receptive than men are, and because they tend to be more "relationship-" than "task-oriented" (for these terms, see Richard R. Gesteland, 1996). But gender is complicated enough in one's own culture – in a cross-cultural setting it is a minefield of possible interpersonal misunderstandings. You may find yourself (as a woman) emancipating yourself in your own culture from a vast ballast of gender prejudices and expectations and then stepping into the social context of an alien cultural environment where these and other, unfamiliar, behavioural expectations are ruthlessly imposed on you.

Two sensitive novels about a Western woman trying to learn to understand Japan appeared within a few years of each other, and with similar titles. Each shows how the relationship between a European woman and a Japanese man comes to end in failure. Oswald Wynd's *The Ginger Tree* (1977) is actually a "Madam Butterfly in reverse" – Mary, the heroine, is "used" by her Japanese lover, Kentaro, and then set up in Japan as his concubine. But he intends her to be only a concubine, not a wife, and he takes her child away from her, in order to have it brought up as a Japanese. Under very difficult physical and emotional circumstances, Mary does everything that she can to survive in Japan, and at least manages to come to final terms with the country and its culture, even though she knows that, despite the understanding she has achieved, she will always be excluded. By comparison, Meira Chand's *The Bonsai Tree* (1983) is more pessimistic, ending with the death of the heroine, Kate, after the breakdown of her marriage.

Wanting to know and feel is not enough. Modern fiction about India, for instance, is full of well-meaning Westerners – especially Western women – who suffer disaster, culminating in rape, or sexual failure, or at least rejection by the Indians they wanted to get to know better and by white expatriates who resent this intention of theirs. The best-known examples are probably Adela Quested in *A Passage to India* and Daphne Manners in the *Raj Quartet*, but many of the Western women in the Indian stories of Ruth Prawer Jhabvala experience similar fates. Jhabvala, the English-language novelist and filmscript writer, was born in 1927 in Cologne, of Jewish-German-Polish origins. In 1951, she married the Indian architect Cyrus Jhabvala, and lived in India for more than twenty years; recently, she has lived mostly in New York. She has written filmscripts for her friends the filmmakers James Ivory and Ismail Merchant, and won the Booker Prize in 1975 for her novel *Heat and Dust*.

Lee, in Jhabvala's *A New Dominion* (1972), is an American girl in India "on a spiritual quest" (or so she is described in the list of characters at the beginning of the book). She meets an Indian boy, Gopi, who assumes that (like all Western women) she is easy and promiscuous. Her hippie clothes also tend to encourage people to make this assumption. She has already been rebuked by an elderly Indian politician, who criticises her appearance and tells her: "I have seen Western boys and girls behaving in indecent manner in public places. It is not only kissing and hugging, other things also" (p. 16). Gopi invites her out to a kebab house, where the staff and the other guests leer and gawp, assuming that Gopi has already seduced Lee, or is just about to do so. She causes a sensation by biting into a chili that he holds out to her (she is probably unaware that such gestures are used in Indian films as metaphors for sexual actions, and have obscene connotations). He tells her that the kebab house is also a hotel, and invites her to view the upstairs rooms with him. At first she refuses, but then assents when he tells her that there is a good view from there – a trick he has learnt from another Western acquaintance. "What it was they saw so much in a view God only knew," he muses (p. 38).

Once they are alone, to his great surprise and indignation she rebuffs his first attempts to touch her.

> "Don't," she said and shook him off with an easy practised movement.
> What next? He felt utterly bewildered. He also felt that he was letting himself down – and not only himself but all the men downstairs whom he knew to be having exciting thoughts about what was going on up here (p. 39).

She is overwhelmed by the view from the window, and has what she thinks is a sort of mystic experience, "at any rate, she felt a great desire to merge with everything that was happening out there – to become part of it and cease to be herself." But Gopi is outraged, and then becomes sulky. Why did she come with him, then? "What opinion did she have of his manhood?" (p. 40).

> What to make of her? A girl who had been brought to a hotel room – had been led upstairs in full public view – and now she said she had been thinking of something else. And this was not an inexperienced, unknowing Indian girl like his sisters, but a Western girl who was travelling all round the world by herself. Everyone knew that Western girls were brought up on sex, lived on sex. She must have slept with many, many men, over and over again. This thought suddenly

excited and enfuriated [*sic*] him. Who was she to push him away? (p. 41).

She is not like those English or American girls who never think of anything other than sex, she says, and, seeing her sitting beside him on the bed, coolly prepared for serious discussion, he believes her. But he doesn't want to admit it: "He wanted to think about her as one thought about these girls; as the people downstairs thought about her."

And then it happens. She looks at him, and sees how oriental, how different, he looks. She wishes that they could understand each other better, but senses that words may not be adequate. She therefore takes off her hippie clothes, and they have sex – for her, rather unsatisfactorily. As she lies under him, suffering rather than enjoying, she considers whether what they are doing is perhaps part of the "merging" she had longed for as she looked out of the window at the view (p. 42).

The sexual encounter between Lee and Gopi is well-observed intercultural comedy. Both the young people are trapped by their stereotypical views of their own and the other's racial and gender roles. Lee feels that she must give herself, and create understanding, if need be by sex rather than discussion; she doesn't want Gopi to think that his stereotype of Western girls as sex-obsessed is true of *her* – and yet her behaviour, in making herself so easily available to him, merely confirms it. She is a prisoner of her hippie ideology; her anti-racism; her confused yearning for something mystical that she thinks India can give her; and her own incoherence. Gopi is also a prisoner: of his inferiority complex towards Western culture; and of his need to assert himself publicly *vis-à-vis* Lee, to have his "manhood" acknowledged and to live up to the expectations of sexual conquest of the white girl that the staff and customers in the kebab house openly reveal.

In this scene, Lee and Gopi, despite becoming intimate for the first time, both fail to abandon their stereotypical race and gender perceptions. Gopi sees for a moment that she is a person, and not just another promiscuous Western girl, but then he lets the cliché take over again and blocks out his perception of her individuality. And at the crucial moment, Lee has sex with Gopi after all, rather than talk to him.

CONCLUSION

Despite Lee's and Gopi's failure, let us assume that men and women of whatever skin colour want to be *people*, not occupiers of a gender or racial role in a game that has more to do with power relationships than with interpersonal discovery. But before that can be achieved, there is still a lot of work to be done in clearing away the discursive baggage of prejudices and stereotypes.

In particular, the linking of gender role and power relations in colonial/postcolonial discourses of racial alterity provides further evidence of how anti-essentialist, how *constructed*, gender is, and how little it need have to do with biological determinism. Neither system is stable – and we are left with the conclusion that people should negotiate their own identities, and try to find their own ways of structuring their relationships with each other.

REFERENCES

Allen, Charles (Ed.) (1983). *Tales from the South China Seas: Images of the British in South-East Asia in the Twentieth Century*. London: Futura Macdonald, 1984.

Baker, Judith. *Love in the China Sea*. Sevenoaks, Kent: Silhouette, 1983.

Brownmiller, Susan (1975). *Against Our Will: Men, Women and Rape*. New York: Bantam, 1976.

Buck, Pearl S. (1952). *The Hidden Flower*. New York: Pocket Books, 1954.

The Camp on Blood Island (1958) (based on the film screenplay by J. M. White & Val Guest). London: Panther, 1959.

Chand, Meira (1983). *The Bonsai Tree*. London: Century, 1984.

Clancy, Tom (1994). *Debt of Honour*. London: Harper Collins, 1995.

Coward, Noel (1932). "Mad Dogs and Englishmen." In: *In Their Own Words: The English – A Self-Portrait*. Ed. Francis Jarman, Gerhard-Dieter Kämmer & David Whybra. Hannover: Schroedel, 1990, p.7 f.

Cronin, Richard. *Imagining India*. London: Macmillan, 1989.

Devereaux, Captain Charles (1889). *Venus in India*. Los Angeles, CA: Hollywood House, 1967.

Forster, E. M. (1924). *A Passage to India*. London: Book Club Associates, 1987.

Gesteland, Richard R. *Cross-Cultural Business Behaviour: Marketing, Negotiating and Managing across Cultures*. Copenhagen: Copenhagen Business School Press, 1996.

Green, Martin (1979). *Dreams of Adventure, Deeds of Empire*. London: Routledge & Kegan Paul, 1980.

Greene, Graham (1955). *The Quiet American*. Harmondsworth: Penguin, 1962.

Haggard, Henry Rider (1885). *King Solomon's Mines*. Harmondsworth: Penguin, 1985.

Hislop, Richard (1979). *A Rose in the Banyan Tree*. London: Corgi, 1980.

Hougron, Jean (1952). *Blaze of the Sun [Soleil au ventre]*. Trans. Mervyn Savill. London: Hurst & Blackett, 1954.

Hwang, David Henry (1988). *M. Butterfly*. Harmondsworth: Penguin, 1989.

Hyam, Ronald (1990). *Empire and Sexuality: The British Experience*. Manchester: Manchester University Press, 1991.

Jarman, Francis. *The Perception of Asia: Japan and the West*. Hildesheim: Hildesheim University Press, 1998.

— . *A Star Fell*. Hildesheim: Cambria, 1998. Second Edition, Hamburg: Libri, 2000.

— . *Writing Asia: The Western Discourse of Asia in Postwar Popular Literature and Culture in English, with Particular Reference to Japan* [microfiche]. Marburg: Tectum, 1998.

Jhabvala, Ruth Prawer (1972). *A New Dominion*. London: Quartet, 1976.

Kipling, Rudyard (1888). "The Man Who Would Be King" (from *Wee Willie Winkie*). In: *The Man Who Would Be King and Other Stories*. London: Pan, 1975, p. 7-43.

Lambert, Eric (1958). *The Dark Backward*. London: Corgi, 1959.

Lartéguy, Jean (1973). *Presumed Dead [Enquête sur un crucifié]*. Trans. Xan Fielding. London: Granada Mayflower, 1978.

Lennon, John. "Woman is the Nigger of the World" (song). Released on a 45 in April 1972 and on the LP *Some Time in New York City* in June 1972.

Lermontov, Mikhail Yuryevich (1839-40). *A Hero of Our Time [Geroy nashego vremeni]*. Trans. Paul Foote. Harmondsworth: Penguin, 1966.

Loti, Pierre [pseudonym of Louis Marie Julien Viaud] (1879). *Aziyadé*. Trans. Marjorie Laurie. London: Kegan Paul, 1989.

— (1880). *Tahiti: The Marriage of Loti [Le Mariage de Loti]*. Trans. Clara Bell. London: Kegan Paul, 1986.

— (1887). *Japan [Madame Chrysanthème]*. Trans. Laura Ensor. London: T. Werner Laurie, [1915].

McClintock, Anne. *Imperial Leather: Race, Gender and Sexuality in the Colonial Context*. New York: Routledge, 1995.

Madama Butterfly (1904) (opera). Libretto by Giuseppe Giacosa & Luigi Illica. Music by Giacomo Puccini. London/New York: John Calder/Riverrun, 1984.

Miner, Earl (1958). *The Japanese Tradition in British and American Literature*. Princeton, NJ: Princeton University Press, 1966.

Morgan, Ted (1980). *Somerset Maugham*. London: Triad/Granada, 1981.

Netzen, Klaus. *Pearl of Blood*. St. Albans: Mayflower, 1975.

Nicole, Christopher (1973). *Lord of the Golden Fan*. London: Corgi, 1974.

— . *The Sun Rises*. London: Hamlyn, 1984.

Prebble, John (1961). *Culloden*. Harmondsworth: Penguin, 1967.

Quayne, Jonathan. *The English Concubine*. London: Corgi, 1968.

Said, Edward W. (1978). *Orientalism*. London: Routledge & Kegan Paul, 1980.

Scott, Paul (1966). *The Jewel in the Crown* (Part One of *The Raj Quartet*). London: Panther, 1973.

— (1968). *The Day of the Scorpion* (Part Two of *The Raj Quartet*). London: Panther, 1973.

— (1971). *The Towers of Silence* (Part Three of *The Raj Quartet*). London: Panther, 1973.

— (1975). *A Division of the Spoils* (Part Four of *The Raj Quartet*). London: Panther, 1977.

Shelden, Michael (1994). *Graham Greene: The Man Within*. London: Minerva, 1995.

Stoler, Ann Laura (1991). "Carnal Knowledge and Imperial Power: Gender, Race, and Morality in Colonial Asia." In: *Gender at the Crossroads of Knowledge: Feminist Anthropology in the Postmodern Era*. Ed. M. di Leonardo. Berkeley, CA: University of California Press, p. 51-101.

Tacitus. *The Annals of Imperial Rome* [*Annales*]. Trans. Michael Grant. Harmondsworth: Penguin, 1959.

Virgil. *The Aeneid* [*Aeneis*]. Trans. Patric Dickinson. New York: Mentor, 1961.

Wilkinson, Theon (1976). *Two Monsoons: The Life and Death of Europeans in India*. London: Duckworth, 1987.

Wynd, Oswald (1977). *The Ginger Tree*. London: Eland, 1988.

FILMS

Braveheart. Dir. Mel Gibson, 1994.
The Crying Game. Dir. Neil Jordan, 1992.
Rob Roy. Dir. Michael Caton-Jones, 1994.

II.

FROM THE DESERTS OF BELGIUM
TO THE JUNGLES OF KOREA

When men define situations as real, they are real
in their consequences
(W. I. and D. S. Thomas, 1928, p. 572)

Let us imagine that a major U.S. or European company has just missed out on the deal of the century with the Japanese (or perhaps the Koreans, or the Saudis). How did it happen? We suspect that it could, at least in part, have been because the Westerners misunderstood their partners, misread their behaviour, or themselves sent signals that were confusing or even offensive. We know all too well that training in intercultural communication could have done a lot to prevent these problems arising. Indeed, with goodwill on both sides and sensible briefing courses and materials, it should be possible to take a large step towards getting the millennium of efficient international cooperation properly under way.

Although this is a hope that I strongly subscribe to, I would nevertheless suggest that it may prove more difficult to realise than we think. Before the knowledge and techniques of intercultural communication can be brought usefully into play, it will be necessary to shed light on attitudes towards the Other that have accumulated over generations, sometimes (as in the case of the Western view of the Arabs) over many centuries. Like Philip Larkin's *Toads*, these squat in the deeper levels of our mental and emotional mindset, fiercely resistant to our intervention and numbing in their effect on our ability to act. Their resilience derives from the circumstance that they are not simply perceptions evolved on an individual personal basis but *cultural phenomena, i.e.,* learned and shared, which meet certain needs of the culture in which they develop. In their most extreme form they may constitute a whole apparatus of beliefs and stereotyping mechanisms, a *discourse,* that provides, within a specific

37

area of experience, a selfconfirming version of reality, but even in less systematic configuration they can create a serious hindrance to understanding of another culture and its members.

Used in this way, the term "discourse" derives from the French poststructuralist philosopher Michel Foucault (1926-84). Foucault's concern was with European social history, and his writings are confusing and highly speculative, but they have inspired a growing body of more empirically-oriented discursive investigations into the mechanisms of intercultural perception and the ordering of power relationships, including, among others, Edward W. Said's *Orientalism* (1978), Hulme (1986) on the European encounter with the indigenous peoples of the Caribbean, Brantlinger (1988) on British imperialist literature, Miller (1985) and Gruesser (1992) on Africa, Tanaka (1993) on the Japanese view of China, Carrier (ed., 1995) on "Occidentalism", and my own study of the Western perception of Japan (1998). Even Goldhagen's controversial book about "ordinary Germans" and the Holocaust, *Hitler's Willing Executioners* (1996), attempts to establish its discursive credentials (Goldhagen, 1996, p. 80). In the following notes, using examples from social history and popular culture, I shall try to pinpoint some of the characteristics of the discursive process.

One important aspect of the problem is that a dubious perception may be lent credibility even over a period of centuries by the "authority" of its originator. To take a non-human example, one of the most famous images in Western art is the exotic beast in Dürer's 1515 woodcut of a rhinoceros. The original animal, a single-horned Indian rhino presented to the Portuguese by Sultan Muzaffar II of Gujarat, had been sent to King Manoel I in Lisbon in 1514 and placed in the royal menagerie (a crude but recognisable likeness of it can still be found in the form of a stone figure on the outside of the Tower of Belém). Manoel dispatched the rhinoceros to Rome as a gift to the Pope, but it perished in a shipwreck on the way. According to F. J. Cole (1953), who made a study of the Dürer rhinoceros and its history, Dürer, who himself never saw the animal, relied partly on second-hand accounts of its appearance (especially on a sketch and description of it by a Portuguese artist) and partly on his own imagination, yet the result is not entirely inaccurate as a rendering of an Indian rhino. However, Dürer added a number of embellishments, in particular a small additional dorsal horn, a feature which was, in Cole's words, "entirely and gratuitously fictitious" (p. 340). The African rhinoceros, which is two-horned, had been mentioned by authors in antiquity (Martial and Pausanias, for example: see S. W. Stevenson *et al.*, 1889, p. 691 f.), had been imported into the Roman Empire as exotic fodder for the games in the amphitheatre, and (no doubt in this last context) had appeared as an occasional motif on both Roman and Alexandrian coins (see Stevenson *et al.*, p. 691 f., and Dattari, 1901, p. 80, no.1231, also Plate XXXII, respectively) – perhaps it was this that Dürer had in mind when he added the second horn to his Indian beast.

Although the African variety of the rhinoceros looks quite different to the Indian, with a front horn that protrudes outwards rather than backwards and without the "armour plate" of the Indian rhino, Dürer's version became so famous that his half-invented creature served as a model for most renderings of the rhinoceros, including some in natural history books, up to the eighteenth century. It would seem that artists, as well as their patrons and publishers, were either unable or unwilling to stop and think about what they were doing. E. H. Gombrich in *Art and Illusion* (1960) takes the saga of the Dürer rhinoceros as one example of the way in which artists, setting out "to make a truthful record of an individual form", begin "not with [the artist's] visual impression but with his idea or concept"; the individual visual information is "entered, as it were, upon a pre-existing blank or formulary", and if this has no provision for information of this kind, "it is just too bad for the information" (p. 62 f.). Drawing on Whorfian linguistics, he suggests that the images of art operate in a similar way to a language, which "does not give names to pre-existing things or concepts as much as it articulates the world of our experience" (p. 78).

A discursive perception of a particular culture or phenomenon may change or evolve, but if it happens it is likely to be in accordance with the ideological needs of the stereotyping culture, or in response to market requirements, rather than the result of the development of a more differentiated and self-critical Awareness of the Other. Much of Western treatment of non-Western cultures has therefore continued to be *unsympathetic or supercilious* towards the latter and *centred on a range of specific Western preoccupations*. The form may vary, but the essentials remain much the same.

The saga of "The King and I" may be taken to illustrate this. In 1870, an English lady named Anna Leonowens published an account of her experiences in Siam (what is today Thailand), *The English Governess at the Siamese Court*, a smug, contemptuous document that paints a picture of the great King Mongkut (Rama IV, 1851-68), one of the most revered figures in Thai history, as a cruel, capricious despot, an elderly Henry VIII with scholarly pretensions. Leonowens makes fun of the manners and English of "[H]is preposterous Majesty" (Loenowens, 1872, p. 212) and of Siamese beliefs and customs in general. In 1872 a second volume appeared, bearing the suggestive title *The Romance of the Harem* (in Britain, more prosaically, *Siamese Harem Life*) and containing similar subject matter. Leonowens's was the only first-hand account of the private life of King Mongkut, but, as a later British employee of the Thai royal family has observed, "we need not believe all that she said; her books, particularly her second one, show that she was gifted with a vivid imagination which at times took charge of her pen" (Malcolm Smith, 1947, p. 42).

It might be thought that Mrs. Leonowens's patronising, very Victorian views on Western relations with traditional Oriental cultures would gradually go out of fashion, but in 1945 the whole story was rehashed (and I use the word advisedly) by the American writer Margaret Landon, who produced a biography based on the original accounts, with "as little change as seemed consistent with the change from a first-person to a third-person narrative" (p. 402). The result is something that is, as she put it, "75 per cent. fact, and 25 per cent. fiction based on fact" *(ibid.)*. Landon had followed the advice of a friend and cut the "geographical, historical, and other padding" *(sic)* in Leonowens's work (p. 400, the words being a quotation from an early review of *The English Gov-*

erness); she concentrates on the dramatic material that purports to document Anna's encounters with the king and his courtiers. Landon's "25 per cent. fiction" can be observed in the additional melodrama and venom that she contributes to the Leonowens narrative in scenes like the following one.

Anna has just confronted the king to plead for mercy for a beautiful young girl, Tuptim, who was caught trying to escape from the royal harem and who is to be whipped. The king is amazed – or embarrassed – by Anna's undisciplined (or hysterical?) behaviour, and laughs at her. Here, first of all, is the original account of the incident:

> Staggering to a pillar, and leaning against it, I stood looking at him. I saw that there was something indescribably revolting about him, something fiendish in his character which had never struck me before, and I was seized with an inexpressible horror of the man. Stupefied and amazed quite as much at finding myself there as at the new development I witnessed, thought and speech alike failed me, and I turned to go away (Leonowens, 1872, p. 28).

And here is the third-person version given by Landon, with her changes and embellishments in italics:

> Rallying her strength, she faltered to a pillar and leaned against it, looking at him. *As her face was stripped of its ordinary patina of polite social intercourse by the sudden impact of his laugh, so also was his by the emotions rampant behind it.* She saw something indescribably revolting in him, something fiendish that she had never seen before. *His sense of decency and justice was gone, swallowed in a bestial need to sate in blood the injured pride of the scorned male.* Anna was seized with an inexpressible horror of him. She was stupefied and amazed, as much to find herself still trembling against the pillar *as at the naked evil she had seen within the King's heart.* Thought and speech had left her. She turned to go (Landon, 1945, p.295 f.).

After this demonisation of King Mongkut, the next stage was to make light entertainment out of the story, in the form of, first, a film, *Anna and the King of Siam* (1946), derived from the Landon book and starring Irene Dunne and Rex Harrison, and then a Rodgers and Hammerstein musical, *The King and I,* which was followed by a film version of the latter (1956), with Deborah Kerr and Yul Brynner in the leading roles. In 1972 the material was finally turned into a television series.

The full-length films are slick and entertaining, but they too exaggerate the importance of Mrs. Leonowens as a civilising (Western) influence on the court of a wayward and petulant (Oriental) king, the earlier film in particular playing down the significance of the great moderniser Mongkut, "the real maker of modern Siam" (Smith, p. 34), and playing up that of his successor, Anna's pupil, Chulalongkorn. While the original story had also been insulting and chauvinistic, it had not trivialised its subject in the way that the films, musical and television series do. The "libel" (Warren, 1980) perpetrated on the memory of King Mongkut has thus flourished for more than a century now, to be supplanted only quite recently by an equally dubious fantasy, that of Thailand as a sex paradise (or hell). What all these versions have in common is their explicit message that Thai institutions, whether they are evil or childish or both at the same time, are not to be taken seriously, a perception of Thailand that becomes easier to understand when it is set in the context of the country's unbroken independence and resistance to Western colonialism. Thailand, albeit less spectacularly than Japan (Jarman, 1998), has been a considerable source of irritation to the West, hence the grotesqueries of the "King and I" genre.

Whereas there may be a set of specific responses to, say, Thailand, India or Japan, deriving from a particular and changing relationship of that culture with the West, these are embedded in, and partly derive from, a far older, *general discourse of the East.* The frequency with which the latter comes into play reflects Western ignorance and indifference towards the non-Western that is itself a characteristic feature of discourse. It has even been possible to make a career in Europe out of looking vaguely "Oriental", evoking a mono-

42

lithic Asian culture that has never existed. In the early years of this century, a Dutch adventuress, Margarete Gertrud Zelle (1876-1917), could successfully pose as an exotic dancer from the Far East, "Mata Hari", with her own imaginative blend of costumes and dance styles (*Illustration 1*).

Illustration 1: Mata Hari (see also Illustrations 2-3)

In the 1980s, a circus with the name Traumtheater Salome ("Salome Theatre of Dreams") toured Europe with shows that queasily combined elements of Ancient Egypt, India and the Arabian Nights. This muddled exoticism would seem to suggest that many people prefer to perceive Asia as a colourful if disturbing fantasy, and may be unwilling to bother with real Asian people and problems, and perhaps incapable of coping when they do encounter them.

Western contempt becomes apparent, for instance, in the marked lack *of interest in maintaining accuracy and authenticity of detail* frequently shown in art, literature, films, and advertising. To take an especially crass example, in the adventure film *Invaders of the Lost Gold* (directed by Alan Birkinshaw, 1982) the hero recounts how he went off into the jungles of Korea – which is rather like talking about the deserts of Belgium or the steppes of New Jersey. Whether such howlers are the consequence of ignorance or indifference on the part of the scriptwriter remains open to debate.

Book illustrations are particularly cavalier in their treatment of Asian ethnography. For example, the same scene of jungle battle graces the covers of two quite different paperback novels about different countries and different wars: *The Dead and the Damned* (no date, but first published in 1967) by W. Howard Baker ("Bill Rekab" on the cover), which is about the American war in Vietnam, and *Bamboo Hell* (1980) by Bernard Finlay, which is about the British fighting the Japanese in Burma during the Second World War. Both novels were published in England, though by different publishers. Perhaps it was felt that the cover of one book about Westerners fighting Asians would do quite nicely for another novel on that subject, and that the picture's basic elements – jungle, water, death, enemy ambush, rescue, clash of races and cultures, openness versus treachery, white superiority – could be seen as satisfactorily typical of both of these Asian wars between white and yellow men.

It is a similar story with advertising. Perhaps it is invidious to single out individual fast food companies for a kind of vulgarity to which most of them are prone, with their "theme weeks" and sudden changes of décor, but not long ago the German Nordsee fast food chain publicised a special

44

Asia Snack Box (note the use of English for the name of the product on offer) containing *Fischnuggets, China-Röllchen und asiatische Sauce*, and advertised this under the feebly-punning, pseudo-Chinese inscription *Hao Rayn* (the German *Hau rein!* means "Get stuck in!") even though the figure in the advertisement was that of a *Japanese* sumo wrestler. McDonald's Deutschland, in a similar campaign, offered what they called *Neues aus Fernkost. Neues aus Fernost* means "Something new from the Far East", but *Fernkost*, a pun on the word *Feinkost* ("Delicatessen"), would suggest roughly "exotic food". The remarkably insensitive television advertising that accompanied this campaign showed Buddhist monks, presumably vegetarian, marching towards a McDonald's sign and chanting not "Om" but "Em" (*i.e.*, "M" for "McDonald's"). The food offered included *Thai Gemüse Rolls* (*i.e.*, Thai Spring Rolls; the mixture of German and English is particularly awkward here), *Singapur Shrimps, Curry McChicken*, and the *Samurai Burger* – under a series of punning slogans in pseudo-Japanese script.

I have taken the liberty of trying to explain them, not an easy task, and must acknowledge the help of my friends and colleagues Rainer Barczaitis, Annette Sabban, and Wolfgang Christian Schneider, who provided all kinds of interesting ideas, some of which have been included here, to help explain what it was that the McDonald's advertising team thought they were up to. It may be an indication of the general standing of the advertising industry, however, that, as with the Devil in the Middle Ages, it is assumed that there are no lengths, however grotesque and far-fetched, to which the hidden persuaders will not go in their efforts to seduce the innocent public. The most significant target group of this particular campaign may well have been the educated middle class, a sector of the German population comparatively resistant to fast food – it is more likely that they would have been tempted, indeed *able*, to work out the puns than that some of the more typical German consumers of this kind of food would have been.

• It starts easily enough: "VOM BANKOCH" is a pun on the name of the Thai capital, Bangkok, and the German word *Koch* ("cook").

• "DEHLI KAT" is a pun on the name of the Indian capital, (New) Delhi, and the German word *delikat* ("delicious"). Perhaps also an echo of "deli" as in "delicatessen" (a word that came into the English language from German).

• "ESS MA PUR" approximates (in very crude German) to something like "Pure eating!" or "Eat it straight!", perhaps with a Bavarian echo to it. Some of my German friends saw here an oblique reference to mum ("ma"), perhaps in the sense of mother being a guarantor of good, healthy food. More obviously, it also reflects the name Eschnapur, the fictitious Indian city that is the setting of a number of German light entertainment adventure films (for more about which, see below).

• "TAKE WAN HOME" combines (1) an exhortation (in English) to take advantage of the McDonald's takeaway service, perhaps with the idea too of there being a particular item ("one") that should be taken home to impress the family with or simply to be enjoyed at greater leisure, with (2) a pun on *taekwondo* (a martial arts discipline from Korea) and (3) a reference to the *wan tan*, a sort of dumpling often encountered in Chinese restaurants. The text seems to play on the common Western misconception that Chinese words are always monosyllabic. Could "wan" also be suggestive of a Chinese name like Wang or Wong?

• "HAI THAI THAI": Apart from containing an obvious reference to Thailand and the Japanese word *hai* ("Yes", although this may simply mean "I'm listening!"), this also reflects the colloquial German expression *Hei tei tei* which approximates to something like "Ooh la la". There may be other connections and associations involved here, for instance with a work *Die Heitherethei und ihr Widerspiel* (1857) by the Thuringian dramatist and novelist Otto Ludwig (1813-65), *Heitherethei* itself possibly being an echo of the erotic cry of *Tandaradei!* in a famous poem by the great German poet Walther von der Vogelweide (c. 1170-1230), *Unter der linden an der heide*. Or there may be an oblique reference to the Korean fabulous beast the *haitai*, which can be seen on the label of grocery products, widely available in Germany, of the Korean food processing company of that name. Finally *tàitai* means "woman" in Mandarin Chinese ("hey, lady!").

There is no systematic correlation between the word-plays in the advertising and the products being offered – the customer is expected to make the connections himself, along the lines of everything Oriental being a reasonable association for everything else. Thus, at the time of writing, a particular brand of savoury snack, Chio's *Asia Snack* (English again!), "*das Knabbererlebnis mit der Faszination Asiens*" – a slogan which sounds just as stupid in English translation: "The nibble experience with (all) the fascination of Asia" – is being marketed in packaging decorated with a Chinese dragon, and with German text in pseudo-Oriental typography – all this, despite the fact that the flavour is *Indisch-Curry* ("Indian Curry"). In this particular market it seems that the consumer is either hugely ignorant of the different Asian cultures, or completely indifferent to them. *Tai-Fun* ("typhoon", but also "Thai fun"?) *asiatischer Snack*, a similarly packaged product from a rival company, funny-frisch (*sic*), also invites the consumer to "discover the fascination of Asia". Yet however witty a few of the individual puns in this kind of advertising may be, they do not invite the consumer to go on a journey of Asian discovery.

The Western projection of a non-Western culture, confused and artificial as it may be, can establish itself so firmly that *the geographical reality finds it difficult to compete against the myth.* An anonymous writer in *The Calcutta Review* in 1859 recounted the story of how an artistically-inclined friend of his in India sent off some sketches to the *Illustrated London News,* "faithful delineations of scenes in Upper India and the Punjaub" which "rendered ample justice to the monotonous sky, the unbroken flats, [and] the lumpy mango-groves", and was horrified to find when they were published that they had been retouched to show "masses of graceful clouds", "ranges of distant hills" and "undulating or boldly broken foregrounds [...] profusely stocked with cocoa-palms". Being "a real artist", who "loved truth too much to admit cocoanuts in that region", he sought an interview with the publisher, who apologised for the clouds and the hills but "stood firm" on one detail: "very sorry, Captain; but, you see, the British public demands palm-trees" (quoted in Stilz, 1982, p. 34). There are palm-trees, too, in the picture of a "Japanese Buddhist temple" from MacFarlane's *Japan* (1852), reproduced in Yokoyama (1987), who observes: "Note pigtails and palm trees. These were also exotic to most Japanese." However, readers in Europe expected such exotic elements to be present in the Western projection of "Asia" as they were familiar with, irrespective of whether or not these elements were appropriate ethnography. Where the scenery actually happened to match up to expectations, the traveller was especially appreciative. Flaubert, travelling in Egypt in 1850, was delighted to discover that the picturesque village of Mahatta was "like an engraving, an oriental scene in a book" (Steegmuller edition, 1972, p. 124). But, on another occasion, he expressed emphatic disappointment at the lack of (anticipated) "oriental splendour" and "oriental colour" (p. 95).

Going beyond a straightforward lack of interest in plausible ethnography there is the *direct unwillingness to even try to reproduce the culture of the Other.* The power of discourse can early be seen in *Der Tiger von Eschnapur* (directed by Fritz Lang, 1958), which was filmed, probably at the cost of great physical inconvenience and expense, in the palaces and temples of the beautiful Rajput city of Udaipur in northwestern India. A lot of trouble was taken to achieve "authenticity", but for the erotic highspot of the film, Sita's dance, there is a sudden dramatic switch from footage shot in the venerable Jagdish Temple to a studio set of monstrous artificiality that supposedly represents the temple interior. Sita, played by the American actress Debra Paget, and wearing Thai-style false fingernails and what looks vaguely like a Javanese costume, performs a dance that is itself a mixture of styles: Hollywood Arabian Nights, Western nightclub, and (perhaps) just a few elements of Indian dance. We are back in the world of Mata Hari. The set is dominated by an enormous female idol modelled on the sensuous Buddhist art of

Ajanta and Ceylon, and having no connection with the Hindu or Jain religious art of Rajasthan.

It is not likely that Lang would have been allowed to film titillating dance scenes in a genuine Udaipur temple, which might explain the use of a studio set; yet all around him he had original material of the highest quality on which he could have based the costumes, dance style and set for this particular sequence. That he should have preferred the fake exotic, while in the midst of the authentic, in what is arguably one of the most picturesque cities in the world, suggests how strong the craving of the Western film public for traditional discursive images of Asia must have been.

Admittedly, Lang's film was itself an anachronism, a remake of the successful prewar version by Richard Eichberg. Eichberg's film is similarly trite, but it sets the equivalent "Indian dance scene" not in a temple itself but in a cabaret theatre with backdrop – which at least puts the kitsch within inverted commas, as it were. The Paget-role was played by a certain La Jana, born Henriette Hiebel.

The cinema-going public of the Fifties had not yet been saturated with television documentary, news and travelogue images of Asia, or completely come to terms with the idea that the era of European imperialism was over. Today, films of this kind, soaked in xenophobia and sexist attitudes, can only be enjoyed as "camp" or "tongue in cheek" entertainment, but they are still produced, and it is not always clear that nothing serious is intended by them. The most successful example of the genre, the Steven Spielberg/George Lucas film *Indiana Jones and the Temple of Doom* (1983), is generally lacking in those touches of humour that signal that self-parody is in progress – compare Harrison Ford's Dr. Jones with Sean Connery's James Bond, for example – and its unsympathetic portrayal of India is so far off target that it seems not camp or parodistic but merely silly. As in *Der Tiger von Eschnapur,* and possibly influenced by it, there is a scene in an underground temple. Frenzied worshippers chant and sway in front of a huge female idol, which is supposed to be the goddess Kali but which looks more like an unsuccessful clay model topped by a Hallowe'en pumpkin mask. In another scene the dinner guests of the Indian maharajah are served with snakes, beetles, monkeys' brains, and soup with eyeballs floating in it, none of them things which have much to do with Indian cuisine (although some of them do appear occasionally in southern Chinese/Southeast Asian cooking, as flavourings, for medicinal purposes, or to improve male potency). The film thus assumes that filmgoers will be broadly ignorant of Asian culture – or that they will be indifferent to a gross travesty.

How offensive a casual attitude to ethnography can be to people from the culture that is being portrayed often only becomes apparent to Westerners when it is their own culture that is being travestied. When the American television version of Herman Wouk's *The Winds of War* was shown on German television in 1986, one reviewer ("E.D.B.") picked out a minor inaccuracy to complain about and then remarked:

> Eine Kleinigkeit? Mag sein. Aber auch ein erster Hinweis auf die anhaltenden Schwierigkeiten Hollywoods (und wohl auch der Amerikaner überhaupt), andere Völker so ernst zu nehmen, dass man sich mit ihnen wirklich befasst. ("A triviality? Perhaps. But also a first indicator of the continuing problem that Hollywood has – indeed, that all Americans have – in taking other races seriously enough to pay proper attention to them")

But it could be argued that, given the pronounced Western tradition of poetic licence in matters of ethnography, the writer was perhaps being oversensitive.

Re-education alone will hardly counteract the ignorance and indifference, or the exoticising tendency, of our (or their) common response to the Other. The problem is that whichever standpoint is adopted, whether Western or non-Western, the more that is found out about *Ausländer, gaijin, farang,* natives, "wogs", and foreigners, and how to communicate and socialise with them, the less suitable they become as a crude out-group. When this happens, the traditional structures of cultural identity begin to totter. As

50

Kipling so perceptively wrote, in *We and They* (*Complete Verse*, p. 631 f.):

All good people agree,
And all good people say,
All nice people, like Us, are We
And every one else is They:
> But if you cross over the sea,
> Instead of over the way,
> You may end by (think of it!) looking on We
> Are only a sort of They!

First there will have to be a substantial change in attitudes, however, because these categories of "We" and "They" are simply too useful for purposes of self-definition to be quickly dispensed with. Whether in books, in films, or in marketing, the cultural mechanisms for maintaining them are still firmly in place.

REFERENCES

Baker, W. Howard. *The Dead and the Damned.* London: Zenith, [1967].

Brantlinger, Patrick. *Rule of Darkness: British Literature and Imperialism 1830-1914.* Ithaca, NY: Cornell University Press, 1988.

Carrier, James G. (Ed.). *Occidentalism: Images of the West.* Oxford: Oxford University Press, 1995.

Cole, F. J. "The History of Albrecht Dürer's Rhinoceros in Zoological Literature." In: *Medicine and History: Essays on the Evolution of Scientific Thought and Medical Practice Written in Honour of Charles Singer.* Ed. E. Ashworth Underwood. London: Oxford University Press, 1953, Vol. I, p. 337-56.

Dattari, G. (1901). *Monete Imperiali Greche, Numi Augg. Alexandrini: Catalogo della collezione G. Dattari compilato dal proprietario.* Bologna: Forni, 1974.

"E. D. B." "Exotisch wie die Deutschen." In: *Hannoversche Allgemeine Zeitung.* January 28, 1986, p. 8.

Finlay, Bernard. *Bamboo Hell.* Bridlington, Yorks: Peter Haddock, 1980.

Flaubert, Gustave. *Flaubert in Egypt: A Sensibility on Tour: A Narrative Drawn from Gustave Flaubert's Travel Notes & Letters.* Trans. and ed. Francis Steegmuller. London: The Bodley Head, 1972.

Goldhagen, Daniel Jonah. *Hitler's Willing Executioners: Ordinary Germans and the Holocaust.* London: Abacus, 1997.

Gombrich, E. H. (1960). *Art and Illusion: A Study in the Psychology of Pictorial Representation (The A. M. Mellon Lectures in the Fine Arts 1956).* Oxford: Phaidon, 1977.

Gruesser, John Cullen. *White on Black: Contemporary Literature about Africa.* Urbana & Chicago, IL: University of Illinois Press, 1992.

Hulme, Peter. *Colonial Encounters: Europe and the Native Caribbean, 1492-1797.* London & New York: Methuen, 1986.

Jarman, Francis. *The Perception of Asia: Japan and the West.* Hildesheim: Hildesheim University Press, 1998.

Kipling, Rudyard. *The Complete Verse.* London: Kyle Cathie, 1990.

Landon, Margaret. *Anna and the King of Siam.* London: Harrap, 1945.

Leonowens, Anna H. (1870). *The English Governess at the Siamese Court: Being Recollections of Six Years in the Royal Palace at Bangkok.* London: Arthur Barker, 1954.

— (1872). *Siamese Harem Life.* British edition (1873) of *The Romance of the Harem.* London: Arthur Barker, 1952.

Miller, Christopher L. *Blank Darkness: Africanist Discourse in French.* Chicago & London: Chicago University Press, 1985.

Said, Edward W. *Orientalism.* London: Routledge & Kegan Paul, 1980.

Smith, Malcolm (1947). *A Physician at the Court of Siam.* Singapore: Oxford University Press, 1982.

Stevenson, Seth W. *et al.* (1889). *A Dictionary of Roman Coins, Republican and Imperial.* London: Seaby, 1982.

Stilz, Gerhard (Ed.). *Grundlagen zur Literatur in englischer Sprache – Indien.* Munich: Fink, 1982.

Tanaka, Stefan. *Japan's Orient: Rendering Pasts into History.* Berkeley, CA: University of California Press, 1993.

Thomas, W. I./Thomas, D. S. *The Child in America: Behavior Problems and Programs.* New York: Alfred A. Knopf, 1928.

Warren, William. "Anna and the King: A Case of Libel." In: *Asia,* 2/6, March-April 1980, p. 42-45.

Yokoyama Toshio. *Japan in the Victorian Mind: A Study of Stereotyped Images of a Nation, 1850-80.* London: Macmillan, 1987.

FILMS

Anna and the King of Siam. Dir. John Cromwell, 1946.

Indiana Jones and the Temple of Doom. Dir. Steven Spielberg, 1984.

Invaders of the Lost Gold. Dir. Alan Birkinshaw, 1982.

The King and I. Dir. Walter Lang, 1956.

Der Tiger von Eschnapur. Dir. Richard Eichberg, 1938.

Der Tiger von Eschnapur. Dir. Fritz Lang, 1958.

Illustration 2: "Dancing-Girl of Cashmere", a wood-engraving book illustration taken from Leo de Colange, *Voyages and Travels*, Boston: E. W. Walker, 1887.

Illustration 3: Nineteenth-century photograph, very likely taken for a European customer, of a *nautch*, or dancing-girl (from Udaipur in Rajasthan).

III.

J. G. BALLARD:
THROUGH THE EYES OF A CHILD

I am not young enough, Crichton, to know everything
(J. M. Barrie, The Admirable Crichton, *1902, Act I)*

The most powerfully written and technically interesting Second World War novel of Japanese captivity is J. G.
Ballard's *Empire of the Sun*, which has enjoyed both popular
and critical success. This semi-autobiographical novel was
published in 1984, and a sequel, *The Kindness of Women*,
with an opening section containing similar material, appeared in 1991. *Empire of the Sun* was filmed by Steven
Spielberg in 1987.

Irrespective of any political or ideological intentions,
Ballard's novel derives great force from the author's involvement with its central figure, the child Jim: ideas about the
war are refracted through Jim's experiences and perceptions.
As a child in China, Ballard watched the most terrible events
unfold, "but through the window of a chauffeur-driven car",
close to the brutalities but unable to do anything about them.
Writing the first book "may [have been] an attempt to go
back and put emotion in". He needed "a very long time, 20
years or so, to forget the events that took place in Shanghai
and [...] a very long time to remember them again [...] to
flesh them out, to remythologise them" (quotations from Angela Carter, 1984, p. 18).

Ballard has claimed that he originally intended to
have an adult central character, but found that "nothing came
alive" until he thought of using a thirteen-year-old: he had
"no adult response to that experience and couldn't imagine
one" (quoted in Martin Amis, 1984, p. 53). This is an in-
genuous explanation, given the subtle effects that the author
manages to achieve by means of this device. Yet whatever
Ballard's reason for writing through the eyes of a child may

have been, the result has been to turn the traditional Japanese POW camp discourse upside down.

In the chaotic, frightening world experienced by Jim, Ballard's young protagonist (in the second book he has become "Jamie"), the Japanese represent order and discipline. Jim admires their military prowess, their bravery, seriousness and stoicism (*Empire*, p. 23; *Kindness*, p. 36). Although "officially his enemies", they offer "his only protection in Shanghai" (*Empire*, p. 60). They are "strong", completely unlike the officers in the British forces and most of the adults in the camp (*Kindness*, p. 58). He identifies himself with a young Japanese pilot, an imaginary twin whom he needs "to help him survive the war" (*Empire*, p. 337) and whom he dreams of flying away with. And yet

> Jim was well aware that his commitment to the Japanese Air Force stemmed from the still fearful knowledge that he had nearly given his life to build the runway, like the Chinese soldiers buried in their untraceable lime pit beneath the waving sugar-cane. If he had died, his bones and those of Basie and Dr. Ransome would have borne the Japanese taking off from Lunghua to hurl themselves at the American picket ships around Iwo Jima and Okinawa. If the Japanese triumphed, that small part of his mind that lay forever under the runway would be appeased. But if they were defeated, all his fears would have been worth nothing (*Empire*, p. 188).

In "the secure world of the camp" (*Empire*, p. 164) Jim enjoys "the happiest year" of his life (*Empire*, p. 180). The camp is "familiar and reassuring" (*Empire*, p. 185), and Jim realises that "inside Lunghua they were free" (*Empire*, p.309). In the later novel, the camp has become Jamie's "entire world" (*Kindness*, p. 37); he is "too wedded to Lunghua to want to leave it", and has found a "special freedom" in the camp that he had never known in Shanghai (*Kindness*, p.48). When the tide of the war turns against the Japanese, Jim is "confused by the collapse of order within the camp" and unwilling to believe that the war might be over (*Empire*, p.

235). Later he is shocked to find the "once immaculate floor of the orderly room, polished by the Chinese prisoners between their beatings, [...] covered with dirt and refuse" (*Empire*, p. 295).

Cruelty is part of the ambience of the novel, and is not specifically associated with the Japanese. A list of the most extreme incidents of physical or mental cruelty in the story would probably include only one (in which a Chinese coolie is beaten to death) that involved the Japanese (*Empire*, p. 228). The other incidents show a Chinese thief trying to cut off Jim's hand in order to steal his wristwatch; the opportunistic Americans Frank and Basie trying unsuccessfully to sell Jim to the Chinese and then telling him that he is worthless; and British camp leaders closing the camp gates on Jim, Dr. Ransome, and other sick and injured prisoners of the Japanese (*Empire*, p. 58, 104, 154). Jamie's last glimpse of China, in *The Kindness of Women*, from the boat that is taking him to Europe, is the grim sight of hundreds of Japanese POWs being herded by their American guards towards Kuomintang soldiers, "bayonets fixed to their rifles", who are "waiting for the *Arrawa* to move away" (*Kindness*, p. 73) – the scene is a little masterpiece of gradually insinuated horror.

Perhaps the most terrifying experience of all, because so unexpected, is Jim's encounter, in *Empire of the Sun*, with the deranged Lieutenant Price, who has already beaten a helpless Japanese to death with his bare hands:

> In the cell at the far end of the yard, shaded by a straw mat hung from the bars, was the body of a dead Japanese soldier. He lay on the cement bench that was the cell's only furniture, his shoulders lashed to the remains of a wooden chair. His head had been bludgeoned to a pulp that resembled a crushed water melon, filled with the black seeds of hundreds of flies.
>
> Jim stared through the bars at the soldier, shocked that one of the Japanese who had guarded him for so many years should have been imprisoned and then beaten to death in one of his own cells (*Empire*, p.296).

Lieutenant Price takes a dislike to Jim.

> Jim stepped back, keeping the silver canisters between himself and this unstable man. As if excited by the booty in Nantao Stadium, the lieutenant's hands were bleeding through their bandages. Jim knew that Lieutenant Price would have liked to get him alone and then beat him to death, not because he was cruel, but because only the sight of Jim's pain would clear away all the agony that he himself had endured (*Empire*, p.298).

These two short texts repay closer examination. There is, first of all, the careful, banal detail establishing the realness of the scene (but with a slight ambiguity: does the mat shade the body from the sun or from human gaze?); the vivid but innocent metaphor; and Jim's disapproval of what has happened, and identification with the dead Japanese. And then in the second quotation the peculiar image of the hands bleeding "as if excited"; the restrained statement of the terrible danger that Jim is in; and finally Jim's compassion for the disturbed man.

The density of ideas and emotions has been achieved with extreme economy of means, and without denying the complexity of feelings going through Jim's mind. The reader benefits both from the child protagonist's lack of experience and from his openness to it. Ballard has been quoted as saying that he was aiming at "an imaginative truth of the world at the time as a boy saw it" (Absalom, 1988), although, reviewing Spielberg's film of the novel, Philip French (1988) pointed out that in both the film and the book "we see more through [Jim's] eyes than he sees himself". The natural reaction of an adult protagonist would more likely have been to evaluate and attitudinise, forestalling the reader's imaginative involvement. For example, Agnes Newton Keith, in one of the best-known autobiographical POW narratives of the Pacific War, *Three Came Home* (1947), describes a similar atrocity, but her throw-away account is merely used as a peg on which to hang her moral commentary: "Confused though our thoughts were as to the ideology of war, I did not believe that we had fought it in order to retaliate in kind for the actions which we condemned" (Keith, p. 307).

The use of a child protagonist also offers an effective means of criticising the behaviour of the Westerners. Jim has neither any ideological commitment, nor personal pride invested in the shattered Western hegemony. To return to Ballard's metaphor: he has always been a passenger in the car, never the driver. Jim is particularly dissatisfied with the British, and fellow-countrymen of his are described as "tiresome", deluded, always complaining, snobbish, "morose and complicated", and contemptible (*Empire*, p. 129, 167 f. and 190, 174, 213 f., 216, 228). Jim's/Jamie's revisionist overturning of the truisms of the war derives at least in part from his tendency to identify with the Japanese. He can see his "own" people with the same contempt that the Japanese feel for them:

However complicated the British at Lunghua seemed to me, there was no doubt that Sergeant Nagata found them infinitely more mysterious, a stiff-necked people whose armies in Singapore had surrendered without a fight but nonetheless acted as if they had won the war (*Kindness*, p. 35).

There is a scene later where Jamie observes the mishandling of English POWs who have been caught while trying to escape. He sees the cruelty, but he also understands how the POWs' frightened bravado is provoking the Japanese, how "to Mr. Hyashi and Sergeant Nagata they were being deliberately insolent in a peculiarly British way, never more arrogant than when they had blundered into defeat" (*Kindness*, p. 46).

Jamie's identification with the Japanese, like his complex attitude towards violence and suffering in general, extends itself beyond the camp years into his later adult life. He watches Japanese soldiers murder a Chinese gratuitously after the war has already ended: none of them are moved by the death, "as if they knew that they too were dead, and were matter-of-factly preparing themselves for whatever end would arrive out of the afternoon sun" (*Kindness*, p. 61). In a reminiscence twenty years later, Jamie compares himself and his friend Peggy Gardner, with whom he shared the experience of Lunghua and who is haunted by "spectres", to the Japanese soldiers: all of them are "trapped by time" (*Kindness*, p. 210). War is a way for nations and people to set themselves free – the four soldiers "had tormented the Chinese to death in the hope that cruelty alone would release the mainspring of war" (*ibid.*).

Partly as a consequence of Jim's/Jamie's preoccupation with the Japanese, there are indications in both books that he is not particularly popular with most of the other POWs. At least one of them, Mrs. Dwight, apparently regards him as an informer (*Kindness*, p. 32). Some of this resentment has now extended beyond the novel, with doubts being cast on the truthfulness of the boy's perceptions. But it could also be argued that when indignant survivors of the camp protested in the British press that "Mr. Ballard was a young boy. He ought to have spoken to people who were a bit older than himself" (quoted in Absalom, *op. cit.*), they were unwittingly confirming the effectiveness of the device of using a child to criticise the behaviour of the adults.

Unlike most of the protagonists of POW writing, Jim quickly abandons any pretence of Western moral superiority. He steals from the elderly (*Empire*, p. 120), and is not displeased when other prisoners die, because this means a redistribution of their property (*Empire*, p. 198). When food runs very short, "Mr. Maxted [catches] Jim looking at the wristbones of Mrs. Hug that had emerged from her grave, as white as the runway at Lunghua Airfield" (*Empire*, p. 234).

Jim is honest with himself. When Japanese soldiers beat a Chinese to death, Jim knows that they are doing it to show their contempt for the British, first for being prisoners, and then for not daring to move an inch to save this Chinese coolie.

> Jim realised that the Japanese were right. None of the British internees would raise a finger, even if every coolie in China was beaten to death in front of them. Jim listened to the blows from the staves, and to the muffled cries as the coolie choked on his blood. Dr.

Ransome would probably have tried to stop the Japanese. *But the physician was careful never to go near the parade ground* (*Empire*, p. 228, my italics).

Jim learns racial humility in the camp, comparing the prisoners' condition with that of the Shanghai beggars (*Empire*, p. 113, 226, 301), and the appearance of the Japanese officers with that of the prewar Westerners: "Their buckles and polished badges shone like the jewellery of the Europeans who had visited the battlefields near Hungjao before the war [to gawp at the carnage and at the dead Chinese]" (*Empire*, p. 160). Through watching Basie, Jim comes to an important moment of self-discovery and self-criticism:

> Sitting beside Basie as he polished his nails, Jim realised that the entire experience of the war had barely touched the American. All the deaths and starvation were part of a confused roadside drama seen through the passenger window of the Buick, a cruel spectacle like the public stranglings in Shanghai which the British and American sailors watched during their shore-leaves. He [*i.e., Basie*] had learned nothing from the war because he expected nothing, like the Chinese peasants whom he now looted and shot. As Dr. Ransome had said, people who expected nothing were dangerous. Somehow, five hundred million Chinese had to be taught to expect everything (*Empire*, p. 322).

The metaphor of the roadside drama seen (with moral and emotional detachment) from a passing car could be applied to most Western experience of Asia. Jamie describes the horrors of Shanghai in the years before Pearl Harbor as "little more than a peripheral entertainment of a particularly brutal kind" (*Kindness*, p. 28). Jim grows up enough to be able to describe Shanghai as a "terrible city" – it is a reasonable assumption that the last words of the book are both Jim's *and* the author's – and to know that, one day, "China would punish the rest of the world, and take a frightening revenge" (*Empire*, p. 351). He finds the body of the young Japanese pilot, which stirs momentarily into life when he touches it, causing Jim to have a vision of resurrecttion transcending racial and cultural barriers. He dreams of being able to raise first the pilot from the dead, and then himself, the millions of dead Chinese, Basie, his mother and father, Dr. Ransome, the British prisoners in hospital and the dead Japanese in the ditches (though not Lieutenant Price or the Chinese bandits) (*Empire*, p. 340). Angela Carter (*op. cit.*, p. 18) has pointed out that *Empire of the Sun* shares the theme of death and resurrection with Ballard's previous major novel, *The Unlimited Dream Company* (1979), "the earlier one in a radiant, visionary mode, the later one as delirious obsession". Some time afterwards, Jim realises that it was probably a different pilot. "All the same, certain events had taken place, and with time perhaps others would have returned to life" (*Empire*, p. 349).

By means of his juvenile protagonist, Ballard can avoid the clichés of emotional description, describing suffering in a detached and unfamiliar way without, however, seeming heartless. It is the reader who is left to "put the emotion in". Jim is often coolly matter-of-fact in the face of suffering, or absorbed in finding answers to practical problems. For example, when his parents run over an old beggar, Jim can see the pattern of the Firestone tyres in his flesh. Even though he feels sorry for the man, he can only think of the patterns – if they had been driving in Mr. Maxted's Studebaker, he reasons, "the old man would have been stamped with the imprint of the Goodyear Company" (*Empire*, p. 36). Jim speculates about such things as whether swimming pools are tiled so that when people are murdered in them the blood can be washed away more easily (*Empire*, p. 66). In the camp, he watches the eyes of the dying, "trying to detect a flash of light when the soul left" (*Empire*, p. 207).

Jim is limited to the metaphors of his childish experience: a wounded soldier has hands "like bloody ping-pong bats", while another holds "a yellow silk glove like those Jim had seen his mother carrying to the formal receptions at the British Embassy" (it is the complete skin boiled off one of his hands in a fire) (*Empire*, p. 48); blood on the wheels of a tram makes it look "as if painted for the annual labour union parade" (*Empire*, p. 57); Sikhs beating Chinese peasants with their staves are "a team of carpet-beaters" (*Kindness*, p. 20);

64

dead Chinese infantrymen, half buried in waterlogged trenches, look to Jamie as if they are "asleep in a derelict dormitory" (*Kindness*, p. 30). Jim is so hardened that he forms metaphors in the other direction, too: the paper petals on the Yangtze, clumped around the swollen corpses washed back up on the shore after a poor Chinese funeral, resemble "the coils of viscera strewn around the terrorist bomb victims in the Nanking Road" (*Empire*, p. 41). If these were the perceptions of an adult, they might easily be seen as an unacceptable aestheticisation of the unbearable. As it is, the device of using a child protagonist creates distance, making it possible for the reader to contemplate the unbearable without embarrassment. It also contributes to the literary effectiveness of the novel. The child's clarity of vision, that of a different sensibility, has a defamiliarising and often poetic effect. Some British readers of *Empire of the Sun* were struck by the novel's "Martian clarity" – the "Martians" in this case being a well-known circle of poets around Craig Raine notorious for writing from a standpoint of exaggerated alienation, like visitors from Mars recording their impressions of the strange planet Earth. Clear-eyed, Jim tries to understand and explain things beyond the normal range of a child.

Ballard's skill becomes apparent when *Empire of the Sun* is compared with other accounts of childhood experiences under Japanese rule. Cécile Drouin's novel *Child of the Red Land* (*L'Enfant des terres rouges*, 1985) is about a little French girl who survives hunger and violence in Hanoi under Japanese occupation. Laurence's account of events, diluted by the trivia of mealtimes, sweets, toys and illnesses and reverberating with self-pity, is that of a small child quite unable to understand what is going on around her. Ernest Hillen's autobiographical *The Way of a Boy: A Memoir of Java* (1993) is movingly written, but young Ernest's perspective on the Japanese is conventional: they are the enemy, to be hated – even though Jesus might have taught otherwise – because of their brutality (p. 63).

The film of *Empire of the Sun* fails to open up a child's perspective on the events as effectively as the novel does. The cold eye of the camera, especially in the hands of a director tempted to exploit the potential of the story for movement, colour and drama, invites the viewer to see the horrors of war and react as he normally would to a newsreel or a war film. Yet ironically Philip French's statement, quoted above, suggesting that the reader or viewer "sees" more than Jim, applies far more to the book, since in the film it is hard to tell what Jim is seeing. The film is *about* rather than *of* Jim, and cannot reproduce the debate going on within him, or his hesitant attempts to make sense of the situations. The techniques used in the film to insinuate a distinctively "Jim viewpoint" – unearthly lighting effects, close focus on Jim's facial expressions, or shooting the action from behind his standing figure – generally fail to achieve this.

There is a scene where Jim, separated from his parents, discovers his mother's footprint in talcum powder spilt on the floor of her ransacked bedroom. Accompanied by insistent music, the camera cuts between the powder marks on the floor (suggestive of rape?) and the changing expression (from interest to relief to bewilderment to alarm) on Jim's face. Jim springs to the window to let the wind destroy the disturbing prints and smears in the talc. If only on a subconscious level, he has reached the same conclusion that the viewer is likely to.

In the novel, on the other hand, Jim at first sees in the dozens of footprints only "his mother's bare feet whirling within the clear images of heavy boots, like the patterns of complicated dances set out in his parents' foxtrot and tango manuals" (*Empire*, p. 62 f.). He notices the smell of strange sweat. Later, continuing his innocent speculation, he traces what he thinks are the steps of a dance and imagines his mother being "propelled by an over-eager partner, perhaps one of the Japanese officers to whom she was teaching the tango" (*Empire*, p. 64 f.). The dance-steps seem to him "far more violent than any tango he had ever seen" (*Empire*, p. 65). Trying them out, Jim cuts himself. The rest is left for the reader to fill in, reaching conclusions that Jim is still too young to reach.

Just as in the film, the device of the child protagonist is also less effective in *The Kindness of Women*. This may partly be connected with the fact that the novel is a first person narrative, reminding the adult reader of the different identity and mentality of the narrator rather than inviting direct identification with the child. For the most part, Ballard is scrupulous in maintaining a consistent juvenile identity for the narrator, but there are hints of commentary here and there from a more mature Jamie, especially in connection with the child Jamie's lack of sexuality: "Later I realised that [Olga] was scarcely more than a child herself" (*Kindness*, p. 11) or "[Peggy] was always trying to wrestle with me, for reasons I was not yet ready to explore" (*Kindness*, p. 33). Herein lies a more specific problem – that the text not only draws attention to Jamie's naïveté, but also makes fun of it. For example, when Jamie sees White Russian girls standing outside a big hotel, calling out to the American and British officers, he guesses rather ridiculously that they have painted their faces because they are "trying bravely to cheer themselves up" (*Kindness*, p. 12); his mother, in response to his curiosity as to what they could be selling, eventually volunteers the information that it is "French and Russian lessons" that they are offering (*ibid.*). However, "French lesson" is a British slang euphemism for oral sex, from the world of prostitutes and their customers, and hardly an expression (in this sense) that a middle-class woman in the 1930s would be likely to use in talking to a small child. This lecherous joke, at Jamie's expense, is therefore between the adult Jamie, or the author himself, and the 1991 reader, and thus over the heads of the characters involved in the scene.

In situations like this one, the reader is invited to laugh at the child protagonist, rather than risk the unsettling, though exciting, effect of alienation to be gained from sharing in the child's experience. In *Empire of the Sun*, third person narrative notwithstanding, the reader sees Jim's/Jamie's world more vividly through the child's eyes. Jim's strange perceptions pull the novel in and out of different genres: POW fiction, horror, fantasy, science fiction, children's writing. The boundaries between them dissolve, shaking the reader out of the complacency of familiar discursive conventions – which is a prerequisite for understanding across cultures. It is a notable achievement, but it is also a reminder that there are pitifully few Western novels about the war against Japan that are able to do this.

REFERENCES

Absalom, Steve. "Royal Film of Hell Camp is 'Nonsense' Say Women." In: *Daily Mail*, March 30, 1988, p. 3.

Amis, Martin. "Ballard's Worlds." In: *The Observer Magazine*, September 2, 1984, p. 53.

Ballard, J. G. *The Unlimited Dream Company*. London: Jonathan Cape, 1979.

— (1984). *Empire of the Sun*. London: Panther, 1985.

— (1991). *The Kindness of Women*. London: Grafton, 1992.

Barrie, J. M. *The Admirable Crichton: A Comedy*, 1902. Web page, <http://www.jmbarrie.net/works/theac10.txt> (Accessed 30.08.2004)

Carter, Angela. "The Inner Spaceman." In: *Time Out*, September 27-October 3, 1984, p. 17 f.

Drouin, Cécile (1985). *Child of the Red Land* [*L'Enfant des terres rouges*]. Trans. Jan Dalley. London: Chatto & Windus, 1988.

French, Philip. "Lucky Jim Shanghai'd." In: *The Observer*, March 27, 1988, p. 40.

Hillen, Ernest (1993). *The Way of a Boy: A Memoir of Java*. Harmondsworth: Penguin, 1995.

Keith, Agnes Newton. *Three Came Home*. Boston: Little, Brown, 1947.

FILM

Empire of the Sun. Dir. Steven Spielberg, 1987.

IV.

USEFUL DETECTIVES

The smallest observation may some day be of decisive
importance
- Gross's Criminal Investigation *(H. R. F. Keating)*

One genre of popular literature which lends itself easily to explorations and perceptions across cultures is the detective novel, when this has a non-Western protagonist or a non-Western setting, or even – as in H. R. F. Keating's Inspector Ghote stories and James Melville's novels about Japan – both. It can also be done with a Western detective in a Western setting. Michael Crichton's Peter Smith, in *Rising Sun* (1992), investigates a murder in the milieu of Japanese businessmen in California; he slips into a *kohai-sempai* (novice-mentor) relationship with the Japanophile detective Connor, and Connor "explains" Japan to him as they unravel the murder mystery.

The advantages of detective novels for intercultural purposes are considerable, including, for instance,

• *motivation*: they provide a reassuringly familiar type of entertainment as well as opportunities for describing an unfamiliar culture and the difficulties of interacting with it;

• *identification*: many readers identify with the detective protagonist by habit – and here is an easy and natural way to ensure reader empathy with the representative of an alien culture;

• *close attention*: readers of detective fiction are accustomed to the idea that a single detail may be the vital clue, and so they will focus with interest on ethnographic material served up in the unfolding course of the plot;

• and *insight*: the "ethnic detective" (Freese, 1992) may solve the crime by a logic or a method unfamiliar to the reader, providing insights into alien cultures and even into what in the academic context have been termed "intellectual styles" (cf. Galtung, 1981). Among others, Freese describes the Talmudic wisdom of Harry Kemelman's Rabbi Small (p.155 f.), Arthur William Upfield's half-aboriginal detective Napoleon Bonaparte (*sic*), who combines Western logic with aboriginal instincts, Tony Hillerman's American Indian detectives, with their different understanding of the relationship between man and his environment, and Keating's Inspector Ghote. For example, in Hillerman's *A Thief of Time* (1988), the Navajo detective Joe Leaphorn brings his Indian culture to bear in his interrogation technique,

> [having] learned early in his career that this Navajo politeness often clashed with white abhorrence for conversational silences. Sometimes the resulting uneasiness caused *belagana* [*i.e., white*] witnesses to blurt out more than they intended to say (p. 184).

In *The Perfect Murder* (Keating, 1964), Inspector Ghote's well-meaning attempts to solve an Indian crime by Western methods are thwarted by the social and cultural complexity of India. When he does solve the mystery, it is because of "a rush of wild, pointless enthusiasm brought on by the coming of the rain" (p. 256) and not by his "cherished efficiency" (p. 255), as learned from a German police manual, the *Criminal Investigation* of Dr. Hans Gross.

Japan is an unpromising setting for murder mysteries. Sano, the seventeenth-century detective in Laura Joh Rowland's *Bundori* (1996), solves his case primarily by genealogical sleuthing, after the *samurai* murderer has provided him with obvious clues that the murders are historically motivated. As far as modern Japanese society is concerned, and as explained in several of James Melville's Superintendent Otani novels, nearly every Japanese murder falls into one of two predictable categories: the spontaneous domestic murder, usually committed by a distraught housewife, and the gangland execution (*The Wages of Zen*, 1979, p. 150; *The Chrysanthemum Chain*, 1982, p. 28 f.). Taken strictly as murder mysteries, the Otani novels are disappointing. The murder cases frequently solve themselves, through a combination of lucky chances, predictable behaviour on the part of the Japanese and the consequent unravelling of a characteristically Japanese net of social connections, obligations and involvements. Instead of pursuing his quarry with ruthless logic, Otani tends to let things take their course. In very Japanese fashion, the plot circles in on its solution rather than approaching it with linear directness. Otani applies nudges or hints to his subordinates and it is often they, or his wife Hanae, or, in *The Chrysanthemum Chain*, the amateur detective Andrew Walker, who bring the plot to its *dénouement*, leaving Otani expressing modest surprise ("It's been a revelation to me [...] It serves me right for trying to play detective", *The Wages of Zen*, p. 209).

In this respect, the Otani novels are reflective of the Japanese distrust of directness, but even this seemingly undramatic approach to detection – haphazard Japanese teamwork rather than magisterial Western sleuthing – offers frequent opportunities for elucidation of an unfamiliar culture. There are unstated comparisons between Japanese and Western cultural phenomena:

As soon as [Inspector Kimura] opened the tall wooden gate, approached the front door and tried it gently he realised that something was amiss, though, for it slid open to his touch. This would have been normal enough by day, but not late at night, especially with the head of the household away (*The Ninth Netsuke*, 1982, p. 78).

Or the comparison may be made directly, but slipped into the narrative in the form of a casual thought or remark, as when Otani's wife disappears unexpectedly:

It really was impossible for Otani to imagine where Hanae might have gone. There was of course no danger involved for a lone woman at night. He had often enough shaken his head in disbelief over the tales he heard about muggings and rapes in the streets of American and European cities. The only women who got into difficulties in Japan in public places were the occasional bar girl or whore at the centre of a drunken quarrel (p. 68).

71

On another occasion, Otani has to stay on to work later in the evening, which he does without qualms because "like every other bourgeois Japanese husband he was sublimely confident that whatever time he arrived home his wife would quickly produce his dinner without complaint" (*Kimono for a Corpse*, 1987, p. 62).

Melville's authorial comments are, for the most part, skilfully introduced into the story in a similar way. For example:

[Otani] was good at [interrogation]. Even among a people whose whole language and psychological conditioning tended them towards allusiveness, hints and evasions, Otani's delicate skill in drifting round a subject, illuminating it now from one, now from another aspect, was remarkable (*The Ninth Netsuke*, p. 133).

Or:

Their clumsy and ludicrous early embraces in the hotel room in Miyazaki where they had spent their honeymoon had awoken in [Otani's wife Hanae] a powerful sexual hunger, and being Japanese, she had never been taught that there was anything wrong about such a thing (*The Wages of Zen*, p. 18 f.).

The greatest danger here is that social phenomena of great complexity may be touched upon but can hardly be explained at length without reducing the pace of the novel to a crawl. It occasionally becomes apparent that the narrative is shying away from detailed discussion of a topic. For example, in *The Ninth Netsuke* Otani warns young policemen not to accept presents or sexual favours from members of the public, because he is aware of the "toughness of the social web of Japan" and the difficulty of freeing oneself from "its clinging demands and compensatory benefits" (p. 82). Melville is addressing here – but without explaining – one of the central issues of Japanese social psychology, the question of *obligation*. In *The Chrysanthemum Chain*, Walker is said to be thoroughly familiar with the term *oya-bun*, "though he would have found it hard to explain the subtle relationship between *oya-bun* and *ko-bun*, patron and dependant, without a long disquisition on Japanese history, religion and psychology" (p. 142), and no further help to the reader is offered.

In his historical novel *The Imperial Way* (1986) Melville goes to the other extreme: here, the cultural matter often seems to be holding up the story. Characters are made to mention "typically Japanese" things like chopsticks and raw fish (p. 58). Descriptive details are elucidated at unnecessary length. Thus Yukichi notices the drab clothes worn by the Japanese women, including the "*mompei* tunics and leggings of countrywomen; the clothes that women even in the cities were nowadays being encouraged by the authorities to wear as a mark of frugality and dedication to the national interest" (p. 114). If the semi-colon (in the place of a comma) is not a printing error, it reinforces the impression that an explanation like this is not really part of the text, but more of an annotation or footnote.

What gives the Otani novels complexity is the presence of foreigners in the plot as suspects or witnesses, so that much of the cultural elucidation can be done in interrogation scenes and take the form of lively dialogue. The main Japanese setting of the books is therefore well chosen: Kobe, the "Chicago of Japan", famous for its gangsters and its large community of foreigners. As Otani's subordinate Kimura self-servingly puts it, "In a busy international kind of place like Kobe you get problems that need special handling. And you need people who get along with Westerners" (*The Wages of Zen*, p. 100).

There are also interesting possibilities in the situation of a Japanese transplanted to a Western environment and plunged into culture shock, as happens to Otani and his wife in *Death of a Daimyo* (1984). Their observations give insights into both cultures. We are told that Otani "seldom pondered about the characteristics of Japanese society" (p.62), but he is forced to by his experiences in England, and through his comparisons we are led to perceptions about Japanese society. For example, Otani is nonplussed at the railway station by the lack of such things as announcements

warning passengers to keep away from the edge of the plat-
form:

> Otani commented on all this to Hanae, who
> merely observed rather tartly that is was no doubt be-
> cause English people were less addicted than Japanese
> to committing suicide by throwing themselves in front
> of trains and did not need to be treated like children by
> being told what to do every minute of the day (p. 92).

And when Otani returns to Japan, we are told not so
much *what* he sees at his police station but rather *how* he
now sees it: "It was the effect of having been abroad that
made him see the familiar office with new eyes, and he was
disturbed by its spartan bleakness" (p. 143).

The reader may learn quite a lot about Japanese life
from detective novels like Melville's – as opposed to more
conventional thrillers like Clare Curzon's *All Unwary* (1997),
which, although it presses all the right buttons of discursive
allusion and intextual reference, including the title of the
novel (derived from the Gilbert and Sullivan light opera *The
Mikado*), merely uses the Japanese as dupes and the Japanese
elements as red herrings – and may be tempted to equate
Otani's culture shock with what might be his own predicament in Japan. But he is unlikely to be led to question his
most basic cultural assumptions. The Japanese characters'
thoughts and motives (including those that are different to
ours) are made transparent. The policemen Otani and Kimura
– the wise but fallible police boss and his smart, clever, over-
eager deputy – are reassuringly familiar figures. Much is
made of the strange habits of *gaijin*, but those that are held
up to ridicule – like the Rev. Willard Goober in *The Ninth
Netsuke* – are the ones who would be found ridiculous in the
West as well.

Although there are superficial similarities between
Death of a Daimyo and Janwillem van de Wetering's *The
Japanese Corpse* (1977), the latter is a far more unsettling
experience for the reader, and shows how effectively the detective genre can be used for purposes of cross-cultural ex-
ploration. Two Dutch policemen, the Commissaris and de

74

Gier, are sent to Japan on an assignment, and we are invited to discover Japan through their eyes. But each of them is shaken to the foundations of his personality and forced to confront his own nature.

Van de Wetering himself spent one and a half years in a Zen monastery in Japan, looking for peace and freedom. Through meditation, he tried to achieve distance to things: "To be detached is to be free" (*The Empty Mirror*, 1972, p.133). He was given a Zen puzzle, or *koan*, to solve. Solving it would bring him a brief moment of insight. He failed to solve the puzzle. Several of van de Wetering's visitors to Japan are also faced with a puzzle, the solution of which leads to self-insight followed by departure.

The narrator of the short story "Visit to a Temple in Japan" (in the German-language collection *Die Katze von Brigadier de Gier*, 1983, translations here by F. J.) comes to Japan full of dislike and fear of the Japanese, engendered by the POW experiences of his father, and by rather clichéd ideas about such things as "that well-known Asian impenetrability" (p.116). On his way to a temple, he is beaten up – for no apparent reason – by two Japanese. Detective Inspector Saito helps him solve the puzzle by bringing him to understand how he himself provoked the attack, through his behaviour towards his expatriate host and the host's Japanese wife. He admits that he has behaved badly, and shows his regret by going to the temple and behaving in a humble manner. The two hired thugs show him the way, greeting him with a bow (not an apology). Afterwards, he finds Saito waiting for him: "I thanked him for the service that he had rendered me. We bowed to each other, and I climbed into a taxi for the station" (p. 127).

Like a Zen master, Saito leads the narrator to self-understanding by setting him questions to which he himself must find the answers. Similarly, the narrator is punished for his wrong behaviour in an alien culture (his friend has adopted Japanese ways) by being given a beating, just as Zen pupils are beaten if they fall asleep or show lack of concentration during meditation. Thus the action of the story may be interpreted on different levels: the events which actually occur to the narrator, the process of self-discovery through discovery of a different culture, and the acquisition of self-insight through Zen seem to be metaphors for each other, or different expressions of the same essential process.

In the short story collection *Inspector Saito's Small Satori* (1985), Saito solves a series of mysterious crimes involving Japanese as well as foreigners. Although he is universally regarded as being extremely clever (which is not necessarily an advantage in Japan), the solutions that he finds are derived less from brilliant ratiocination than from Saito's understanding of Japanese culture and (most of all) from his knowledge of a classical Chinese text on detection and jurisprudence, *Parallel Cases Under the Pear Tree* (p. 35, 57, 74, 140, 192). Several of the cases force Saito into self-scrutiny, especially the first case in the collection, in which Saito in a flash of insight realises the meaninglessness of his ambitions (p. 26), and the last, in which he hovers on the brink of abandoning his career (p. 204 f.).

The assignment that the Commissaris and de Gier are faced with in *The Japanese Corpse* (1977) is also a *koan*, a puzzle that leads to unexpected insights. Superficially, the novel seems to follow a traditional pattern. De Gier considers what he knows about the Japanese, and comes up with a mixture of images that suggests cultural schizophrenia: *kamikaze* pilots, brutal POW camp guards, decorative temples and eerie music, Buddhist compassion and equanimity, obedient human insects. "He shook his head. A pilot killing himself while killing hundreds of others, a guard beating prisoners to death, a temple drum splitting the silence. Did he know any more about Japan?" (p. 15). The Dutch ambassador to Japan tells the Commissaris that Japan "is perhaps the most interesting country in the world. Exotic, mysterious and efficient, an unbelievable combination" (p. 58). In the course of the novel we learn that the real villains are the Communist Chinese (who are supplying the smuggled heroin), and not the Japanese. Like Bond in *You Only Live Twice*, de Gier is still in Japan after the adventure has ended, wanting to stay, but likely to go back to Europe after all – "soon" (p. 261).

However, nothing is quite what it seems, and van de Wetering plays with the reader's willingness to impose discursive stereotypes on events and situations. The suspected murderers turn out to be gangsters on holiday. The former victim of Japanese internment admits that she "wouldn't really have wanted to miss the experience" (p. 131). The Daimyo, the "villain" of the novel, is a *kamikaze* pilot who got himself drunk rather than die. The Commissaris had expected him to

> look like an evil wizard, a necromancer with a high pointed hat and a gown reaching to the floor and a staff with a bat's head for a knob. But the man looked fairly ordinary. If it hadn't been for the eyebrows he would have looked like many men the commissaris had met in the streets of Tokyo and Kyoto. A director of a commercial firm or a lawyer or even a doctor perhaps (p. 224).

The nightclub musicians live in a temple. The chief thug turns out to be a bird-fancier, who "isn't as wicked as he pretends to be; he is really very sensitive" (p. 180). The Japanese secret policeman Dorin, on the other hand, proves to be a hate-filled potential Fascist, who is prepared to use illegal methods and is paranoid about Russian invasion. In the moment when Dorin reveals his hatred and viciousness, he is described with direct reference to the discourse:

> Dorin's furious face, each facial muscle working, the gleaming teeth and the wildly gesticulating hands had reminded him of a prewar cartoon, showing a Japanese soldier and warning against the Yellow Peril that was about to attack the world. The soldier had been grinning evilly and had pointed his bayonetted rifle (p. 229).

Yuiko, the girl who entices de Gier, has un-Japanese straight legs and large breasts. Many of the Oriental sex-objects in Western novels and films have Western features, and Yuiko seems initially to be one of these discursive sex-dolls – but her breasts are probably inflated with compressed air and her teeth are capped. Her artificiality is an acidic comment on the false, chauvinistic way in which Oriental sexuality has often been constructed by Western writers.

There are boxes within boxes. The story of the Daimyo's *kamikaze* career is "a good tale, even if it isn't true, but maybe it is true" (p. 212). The threatening message sent to Dorin has, according to Dorin, been written by a foreigner who can read and write Japanese (p. 138 f.). Later, the Daimyo explains that it is a copy by a Japanese of the calligraphy of a foreigner. "You were ninety-eight percent right" (p. 221).

Dorin has an understandable personal reason for hating the *yakuza* – his brother is a heroin addict – but he is susceptible to their charm and has to keep reminding himself what they are like (p. 246). The Commissaris also has to remind himself that the Daimyo "is to be detested. Undoubtedly he destroys the order of the state" (p. 252). But immediately he asks himself why such a man, whom he has already described as "sensitive and intelligent" (p. 250), should do such things, and admits that he likes him very much *and has got to know him*. He senses that the fact of the Daimyo's existence might mean that he plays a necessary role in Japanese society (p. 246). Moments before the Daimyo's brutal death, the two men are "holding each other, sobbing with pleasure and rubbing their heads together in inane and complete surrender to a shared moment of insight" (p. 257). This is the crowning irony of the novel: that the great moment of cross-cultural rapport should be between the hunter and his quarry.

The Commissaris is receptive to Japan more or less immediately. After the initial bewilderment, induced by "the jumble of new images which were forced on his brain" (p.96), his mind

> seemed ready to accept the strangeness and even to rest in it, as a show put up for his entertainment and imagination. He was no longer intent on trying to understand, but was allowing his mind to receive the impressions and to enjoy the colors and shapes and sounds (p. 96 f.).

Nevertheless, he feels that he is "beginning to understand the Eastern mind" (p. 155). The Daimyo tells him that they have both "cleared" their minds, and that "the Buddha mind is empty, empty and pure, for emptiness is always pure" (p. 240). This is essential if one is to try and understand another culture:

> You are in a foreign country and you receive many impressions, words, ideas. All day they fall on you, like raindrops, and like raindrops they roll away down the protection of your mind and are sucked up by the ground. [...] [But] two men will only be able to really meet after they have learned to destroy their own desires (p. 241).

The Daimyo invites him to come and stay with him: "perhaps we can do some traveling and you can tell me what you see and I will experience my country through your eyes. It will be an adventure we can share" (p. 249).

De Gier also warms to Japan very quickly (p. 83 f., 86). His mind has been cleared: he has been shocked out of "caring" about commitments and responsibilities by the sudden death of his girlfriend and by having to shoot his pet cat. He is a "free man [...] shocked out of having to carry the weight of his own identity" although "it's dangerous to be free, to stop caring" (p. 88). It's "asocial" and "abnormal": "A normal man cares" (p. 127). He is not frightened by the threatening charade of his own death. Hardly anything touches him. De Gier is empty, simply a mirror to things that reflect in him and then disappear, leaving him empty too (p.116).

The idea is an important one in van de Wetering's work. In his memoir *The Empty Mirror*, he recounts how a Buddhist hermit told him the story of the mirrors that reflect each other, as all things do: "Everything is connected with everything" (p. 123). His reaction to this is that all the mirrors are empty and that there are no reflections. His mentor Peter tells him kindly that if he could really understand the "empty mirror", he would no longer need to look further (p. 124). The mirror is a famous symbol of Buddha-mind, empty and marvellous. Perhaps Peter is trying to hint to him that there is a contradiction between the phenomenon itself and intellectual awareness of it as an idea, mind giving itself substance while asserting its own emptiness.

The climax of *The Japanese Corpse* now approaches. De Gier feels "supremely alone", increasingly aware of his "utter freedom" and of the fact that he is a foreigner, a *gaijin* (p. 235). The feeling of aloneness and foreignness is a necessary part of being able to perceive an alien culture, but the most important perceptions follow from self-scrutiny. Japan is ideal for this purpose, for, as Ian Buruma (1984) has pointed out, "living in Japan as a *Gaijin* (literally 'outside person') means being a constantly scrutinized odd man out. As a result one cannot help but scrutinize oneself" (p. xi-xii).

Looking at the Daimyo, de Gier is reminded of the figure of a fat little Chinese god in his favourite Amsterdam restaurant, a little god showing cunning and indifference: "An indifference based on insight into a mystery which de Gier [...] had often approached but never grasped" (p. 217). His freedom is created accidentally, but de Gier doesn't know what to do with it (p. 246). Nevertheless, it is a *free* choice that he makes to return to Amsterdam and reassume his identity, after his friend Grijpstra has offered him a new set of reasons for "caring": a new fuchsia for his balcony, lamb in the freezer, a new cat. These are the sort of things that are important to de Gier, and which make up his cultural identity, but he has had to go to the other side of the world and confront himself in the setting of a totally alien culture in order to rediscover this. This is the ultimate usefulness of cross-cultural understanding – that in the end it brings us back, suitably wiser, to ourselves.

REFERENCES

Buruma, Ian (1984). *A Japanese Mirror: Heroes and Villains of Japanese Culture*. Harmondsworth: Penguin, 1985.

Crichton, Michael. *Rising Sun.* London: Arrow, 1982.

Curzon, Clare (1997). *All Unwary*. London: Warner, 1998.

Fleming, Ian (1964). *You Only Live Twice*. London: Pan, 1965.

Freese, Peter. *The Ethnic Detective: Chester Hines, Harry Kemelman, Tony Hillerman*. Essen: Verlag Die Blaue Eule, 1992.

Galtung, Johan. "Structure, Culture, and Intellectual Style: An Essay Comparing Saxonic, Teutonic, Gallic and Nipponic approaches." In: *Social Science Information*, 20, 6 (1981), p. 817-56.

Hillerman, Tony (1988). *A Thief of Time*. New York: Harper, 1990.

Keating, H. R. F. (1964). *The Perfect Murder*. London: Hamlyn, 1980.

Melville, James (1979). *Wages of Zen*. New York: Fawcett Crest, 1985.

— (1982). *The Chrysanthemum Chain*. New York: Fawcett Crest, 1986.

— (1982). *The Ninth Netsuke*. London: Dent, 1986.

— (1984). *Death of a Daimyo*. London: Dent, 1986.

— (1986). *The Imperial Way*. London: Methuen, 1987.

— (1987). *Kimono for a Corpse*. London: Headline, 1988.

Rowland, Laura Joh (1996). *Bundori*. London: Headline, 1997.

van de Wetering, Janwillem (1972). *The Empty Mirror: Experiences in a Japanese Zen Monastery [De Lege Spiegal]*. Trans. J. v. d. W. London: Routledge & Kegan Paul, 1973.

— (1977). *The Japanese Corpse*. New York: Pocket Books, 1978.

— (1983). "Tempelbesuch in Japan." In: *Die Katze von Brigadier de Gier: Kriminalstories [De kat van Brigadier de Gier]*. German Trans. Erwin Peters *et al*. Reinbek: Rowohlt, 1984, p. 112-27. (*Not* in the volume published in the U.S. as *The Sergeant's Cat and other Stories*.)

— (1985). *Inspector Saito's Small Satori*. New York: Ballantine, 1987.

V.

KIPLING'S EXTREMELY DISAGREEABLE STORY

It isn't the kind of story that you would read to your daughter at bedtime.

The plot could be summarised as follows: S, F and K – all hardworking expatriate professionals living and working abroad – meet to celebrate New Year at their club. F in particular drinks too much, and S and K have quite a business trying to get him back to S's place, where he is staying over the holiday. On the way, he breaks away from them, charges into a "native" church, pushes past the priests, and stubs out his cigar on the face of Jesus over the altar. Then he makes himself comfortable on the floor and announces that he wants to spend the night there. There is a god-awful fuss, of course, but suddenly a strange creature appears, a sort of Quasimodo-creature that the priests have allowed to live in the church. He throws himself onto F, and the priests go very quiet. One of them tells S and K to take their friend away, but warns them that although F may have finished for the night, the Lord Jesus has not finished with *him*.

On the way back to S's house, F becomes quite ill. S and K put him to bed and then talk about what has happened. S, who works for the security services, is puzzled that the priests didn't make more of the matter.

When they meet up next morning, F is behaving strangely, demanding raw meat and complaining of having been bitten very savagely by mosquitoes during the night. Indeed, there is a peculiar mark on his chest. To pass the time, they go to admire the horses in S's stables, but the horses panic when F comes near. That evening his behaviour becomes even stranger – he rolls in the earth, howls like a wolf and foams at the mouth. He has become a beast. S and K tie him up, and send for D, the doctor. The doctor declares that it is a terminal case of rabies; there is nothing that can be done.

After the doctor has gone, S reveals his suspicion that it is all somehow connected with the incident in the church. They hear animal cries from outside the house, and every time that it happens, F goes into violent convulsions. It is as though something is trying to take his life. S and K go out into the garden and catch the Quasimodo-creature. They are resolved to force him to release his hold over F, if necessary by torturing him. And it indeed proves to be necessary to use torture.

At dawn the creature finally gives in and frees F of the evil that has had him in its grip. Slowly, F recovers and becomes a human being again. They allow the creature to go. The doctor reappears, expecting to have to record a death, and is amazed to find F fit and well. He leaves, quite offended in his professional dignity. S goes to the church, to offer redress for the damage, but the priest claims that he is unaware that anything has happened. S and K are upset and ashamed of what they have done, but have no logical explanation for the events, and F, who doesn't remember anything at all, can't understand what the fuss is all about.

This, as some readers may have recognised, is more or less the plot of Rudyard Kipling's short story "The Mark of the Beast", from the collection *Life's Handicap* (1891). But less rather than more, because some very important elements have been left out or changed. The Kipling story is set in British India, and Strickland ("S"), the narrator ("K") and Fleete ("F") are members of the governing colonial elite, and white men. The priests and the "Quasimodo-creature" are Indians. The church is actually a Hindu temple, and the sacred image is not of Jesus but of the monkey-god, Hanuman. The "creature" is a leper, whose body has already been badly damaged by the disease.

Many readers of the story have disliked it. Reportedly, when an early draft was sent to the eminent writer Andrew Lang in London he found it "extremely disagreeable" (Lycett, 1999, p. 145). The problem is not so much the element of "devils, bogeymen and things that go bump in the night – Indian-style" – that, after all, is a reasonably familiar genre, and many writers on India have been moved by what they experienced there (or heard about from others) to probe

84

into these murky matters. Kipling himself wrote several other ghost or horror stories set in India, including "At the End of the Passage" (in the same collection), which because of its psychological insinuation is genuinely frightening, and "Beyond the Pale" (in *Plain Tales from the Hills*, 1888), which is shocking because of its sudden brutality. As the narrator in "The Mark of the Beast" explains, "East of Suez" man is "handed over to the power of the Gods and Devils of Asia", a state of affairs which "accounts for some of the more unnecessary horrors of life in India" (p. 208), the *necessary* horrors presumably including such items as the routine exposure to filth, disease and a difficult climate.

Nor is the story "disagreeable" because of any explicit descriptions of cruelty. The means used to torture the leper are mentioned beforehand – "red-hot iron" (p. 221) in the form of heated gun-barrels – and after the event – a "whip that had been hooked round his body" (p. 222) – but in-between there is a row of six little dots where the account of the torture could be expected to be, preceded by the laconic statement: "This part is not to be printed." The cruelties are therefore left to the reader's imagination.

The sensitive reader may therefore want to skip the following paragraph.

*   *   *   *   *   *

It should be pointed out that the true dreadfulness of the situation is barely hinted at in the story, and is not likely to be picked up by someone with no experience or special knowledge of lepers. It is the problem of *how* to torture a leper, much of whose flesh is without feeling. Kipling would have known this, and some of his readers in India would also have known it. Modern readers, fortunately, aren't normally aware of such things. The thought of Strickland and the narrator having to probe the leper's body, to find out which parts are still sensitive, is truly disgusting. It is no wonder that the two men react hysterically when the horror is finally over.

*   *   *   *   *   *

The imaginative reader may share the disgust felt by Strickland and the narrator, but for many the nastiness of the story can be explained straightforwardly enough in terms of its portrayal of colonial and racial brutality, with arrogant white men torturing a poor, sick, non-European who really ought to be in hospital. "The Mark of the Beast" *can* be read on this level, but there are two things that undermine this conventional, politically correct interpretation, and both of them stem from the fact that Kipling is a more complex and a deeper writer than he is generally believed to be.

First of all, Kipling was not a racist (if what we mean by a racist is someone with chauvinistic colour prejudice). Kipling *did* have strong prejudices, for example against Liberal and Radical politicians, and he clearly regarded the races of the world as unequal, with certain races more gifted in particular directions. However, white people were not *per se* superior, although the British had a gift for empire (just as the Germans *didn't*; the Americans, as Kipling indicated in his famous poem "The White Man's Burden", 1899, still needed to learn, and the poem offered them some practical advice on the subject). The much quoted and supposedly incriminating phrase about "lesser breeds without the Law" (*Complete Verse*, p. 266) in another famous Kipling poem, "Recessional" (1897), is, as George Orwell robustly put it, "always good for a snigger in pansy-left circles" but "refers almost certainly to the Germans" (Orwell, 1945, p. 71). Kipling travelled widely in India, mixing (as far as we know) quite happily with Indians. He was capable of adopting surprisingly relativistic positions on occasion, as in the late poem "We and They" (*Complete Verse*, p. 631 f.), or when he told off a leading U.S. Presbyterian in 1895:

It is my fortune to have been born and to a large extent brought up among those whom white men call "heathen"; and while I recognise the paramount duty of every white man to follow the teachings of his creed and conscience as "a debtor to do the whole law", it seems to me cruel that white men, whose governments are armed with the most murderous weapons known to science, should amaze and confound their fellow creatures with a doctrine of salvation imperfectly understood by themselves and a code of ethics foreign to the climate and instincts of those races whose most cherished customs they outrage and whose gods they insult (quoted in Gilmour, 2002, p. 81 f.).

These are hardly the words of a racist bigot; and with regard to "The Mark of the Beast", it has often been overlooked, what with all the attention being paid to the nasty behaviour of the white men, that Fleete is punished most brutally for being unkind not to a *person* but to a heathen idol. It is true that he escapes with his life and sanity intact, but it is a close-run thing, and his two friends pay a heavy emotional price for helping him.

Nor is there any diminution of the dreadfulness of what Strickland and the narrator do to the leper by such devices as dehumanising and objectifying him, techniques that will be familiar from popular novels, comics and films in which the enemy happen to belong to a different race. The leper remains a human being, a "he", not an "it", and the only "beast" in the story is Flete. The leper's humanity is underlined by the name that he is given, the "Silver *Man*" (my emphasis), and although it would be unwise to stretch the symbolism too far, the leper is, by virtue of his disease, *white-skinned* – "his body shone like frosted silver, for he was what the Bible calls 'a leper as white as snow'" (p. 210 f.; the Biblical reference is to 2 Kings 5:27) – and so the situation of torture cannot be conveniently reduced to the now paradigmatic one of colonial white man abusing colonised black.

There is a second reason why a conventional reading of "The Mark of the Beast" is inadequate. Kipling traces within the few pages of this story a horribly difficult but completely topical moral dilemma. Are there circumstances under which it is right to torture a human being?

The decent, liberal answer is "No". Torture is revolting, aesthetically disgusting, and in the ethical systems to which most Westerners subscribe morally wrong. There is also a commonsense reason to avoid it. Torture is a slippery slope down which a culture may slide into ever-increasing brutality as the constraints of law are relaxed or suspended.

Torture as a response to terrorism can produce a vicious circle of accelerating lawlessness and violence. Torture is the "cancer of democracy":

> Can a great nation, liberal by tradition, allow its institutions, its army, and its system of justice to degenerate over the span of a few years as a result of the use of torture, and by its concealment and deception of such a vital issue call the whole Western concept of human dignity and the rights of the individual into question? (Vidal-Naquet, 1963, p. 15).

Of course not.

And yet...what do you do, for instance, if you have in your power the only man who knows the location of a bomb that will soon go off, killing dozens or even hundreds of innocent people? What do you do with a prisoner who knows the whereabouts of hostages whose throats will be cut at midnight? Do you torture him, weighing his pain against their lives (and finding it lighter)? And what if those potential victims or hostages are children, your own child perhaps among them? What do you do? Discussing the taboo on torture, Mark Bowden (2003) has commented: "Few moral imperatives make such sense on a large scale but break down so dramatically in the particular" (p. 9).

A few years ago this would have been no more than an unreal situation, an exercise for an ethics seminar or a topic for a debating society. But now the taking and video-taped murdering of hostages has become almost routine in Iraq, and I write this, on the eve of the anniversary of 9/11, as the dead children of Beslan are being buried. Hundreds of schoolchildren had been held hostage by terrorists, who had factored into their plan the likely deaths of many of their prisoners, had stood by as desperate children drank their own urine, had shot a little boy for talking out of turn, had knifed an eighteen-month-old baby, and had finally shot dozens of children in the back (one girl forty-six times) as they tried to escape. The next horror on this scale has probably already been planned and next time it may not be the Caucasus, but somewhere much closer to the heartlands of the "civilised"

West, where such things are not supposed to happen. Next time, it could be *your* friends or neighbours or children who die. The question is impossible to suppress: If you could prevent such an atrocity by torturing information out of a captured terrorist or killer, would you do it?

What seemed at the time to be a real situation of this kind, albeit on a more intimate scale, occurred in Germany in 2002, when little Jakob von Metzler, son of a wealthy Frankfurt banker, was kidnapped and held to ransom. The kidnapper was captured. Hoping to save the little boy, the deputy police chief of the city ordered that the man be threatened with physical violence. The kidnapper then confessed, but the boy had already been killed. The policeman was suspended, and will soon be put on trial. If the debate in Germany over this episode is anything to go by, many Germans adopt a resolute moral position on the issue. According to an opinion poll published in the popular magazine *Stern*, 63% of those asked whether the policeman should be punished answered "yes" (Elendt & Weitz, 2003, p. 57). No violence had been used, and some fellow policemen saw what had occurred as being part of a "good cop, bad cop" interrogation routine, but the police trade union and Amnesty International both condemned the senior policeman, and AI "expressed the hope that the verdict of the court would make it unmistakably clear that torture was forbidden under all circumstances and without restriction" (Anonymous, 2004).

The willingness of many Western Europeans and North Americans to hold on to what is legal or abstractly "right" even at the expense of pain and heartbreak can be explained in sociological terms – these are "universalist" rather than "particularist" cultures. The paired terms originate from Talcott Parsons's scheme of Pattern Variables (see Parsons, 1951) and are used in intercultural communication to define one of the "cultural dimensions" by which cultural differences can be described. For universalists, rules, laws and moral abstractions indisputably count for more than relationships, social commitments and personal feelings, an attitude that many (particularist) non-Westerners find incomprehensible (if your friend is in trouble, *of course* you try to help, even to the extent of intervening in a corrupt manner, breaking the law, lying in court, and so on). There is an entertaining discussion of this phenomenon in a recent book by Trompenaars and Hampden-Turner (2000, p. 13 f.) on cross-cultural management, with examples that American readers will appreciate immediately, for instance, the predicament of Sheriff Will Kane in the 1952 Western *High Noon*. Germans might in any case be expected to be more inflexible in their attitudes – their reactions to a situation that cries out for a *situational* response – for a reason that is connected with another cultural dimension, that of "uncertainty avoidance" (the term derives from American organisation sociology but was popularised by the Dutch business communication expert Geert Hofstede). Far more so than the "low uncertainty avoidance" Americans and British, Germans (and the French) prefer clear-cut situations, certainty and predictability. To take a spectacular recent example, in the matter of Saddam Hussein's weapons of mass destruction the French and Germans were less willing than the Americans and British to accept circumstantial evidence and calculations of probability as arguments for launching an attack on Iraq. The "old Europeans" stuck with their legal principles for the determining of guilt and demanded to see the smoking gun; they were only willing to consider taking action after the facts had been fully revealed, which would make their moral position unassailable; the more pragmatic Anglo-Saxons argued that by the time there was a smoking gun the disaster would already have happened, and that it was necessary to move quickly to prevent that danger. Who was actually in the right is irrelevant here, because what matters is that both parties viewed each other as irresponsible and reprehensible. To say that *both* views can be seen as correct – that something can be simultaneously right *and* wrong, good *and* bad, grey rather than black or white – is itself a low uncertainty avoidance attitude.

In "The Mark of the Beast", Kipling's torturers know very well that they are doing something wrong and shameful, but their personal loyalty to Flete overrules this sanction. Their behaviour under extreme stress is particularist, possibly, just possibly, because they have been exposed for many years to the ways of a particularist culture (India). Strickland,

90

the policeman, "knows as much of natives of India as is good for any man" (p. 208) and "hates being mystified by [them], because his business in life is to overmatch them *with their own weapons*" (p. 211 f., my emphasis). When the sufferings of Flete become too much to bear, Strickland tells the narrator that he will *take the law into his own hands*, and orders him to help (p. 219). For so much particularism, there will be a legal and a personal price to be paid. As Strickland admits, after the torturing is finished, "[...] I've done enough to ensure my dismissal from the service, besides permanent quarters in a lunatic asylum" (p. 222).

What has happened here is that by means of a kind of existential transaction, the dilemma of torture has been cut like the Gordian Knot. Discussing an even more drastic situation, Albert Camus (1951) describes the metaphysical rebel, the terrorist who kills a guilty man – and only a guilty one, never the innocent: "If Dubassov is accompanied by his wife, I shall not throw the bomb", the anarchist Voinarovsky says (p. 138) – but who then accepts responsibility for his action and willingly pays the price:

> [...] while recognising the inevitability of violence, [they] nevertheless admitted to themselves that it is unjustifiable. Necessary and inexcusable, that is how murder appeared to them. Mediocre minds, confronted with this terrible problem, can take refuge by ignoring one of the terms of the dilemma. [...] A life is paid for by another life, and from these two sacrifices springs the promise of a value (p. 138).

In the interests of civilisation, torture must of course remain forbidden. Occasionally, in the name of compassion – to prevent greater human suffering – it will be used illegally, and in such cases the torturer will have to plead guilty, citing necessity, not as a defence but as mitigating circumstances, and hope for the mercy of the court. With great perception, Kipling takes his two characters, Strickland and the narrator, through such a situation of horror and madness to their own particular existential transaction, by the terms of which, although they have saved the life of their friend, they stand condemned in the court of their own honour. They pay a heavy price (or what in Kipling's time and to someone with his views and beliefs would have seemed a heavy price), for they have "disgraced [themselves] as Englishmen for ever" (p. 223).

References

Anonymous (2004). "Frankfurter Polizeivize angeklagt." In: *Netzeitung*. Web page, February 20, 2004,<http://www.netzeitung.de/deutschland/274225.html>(11.09.2004)

Bowden, Mark. "The Dark Art of Interrogation." In: *The Atlantic*. Web page, October 2003, <http://www.keepmedia.com/pubs/TheAtlantic/2003/10/01/377262?> (Accessed 11.09.2004)

Camus, Albert (1951). *The Rebel [L'Homme revolté]*. Trans. Anthony Bower. Harmondsworth: Penguin, 1962.

Elendt, Gerd/Weitz, Regina. "Wie in der Bananenrepublik." In: *Stern*, February 27, 2003, p.56 f.

Gilmour, David. *The Long Recessional: The Imperial Life of Rudyard Kipling*. London: John Murray, 2002.

Hofstede, Geert/Hofstede, Gert Jan. *Cultures and Organizations: Software of the Mind – Intercultural Cooperation and Its Importance for Survival*. Rev. and exp. ed. New York: McGraw-Hill, 2005 (some earlier editions appeared under the title *Culture's Consequences*).

Kipling, Rudyard (1888). *Plain Tales from the Hills*. London & New York: Macmillan, 1892.

— (1891). *Life's Handicap, Being Stories of Mine Own People*. London & New York: Macmillan, 1892.

—. *The Complete Verse*. Ed. M. M. Kaye. London: Kyle Cathie, 1990.

Lycett, Andrew. *Rudyard Kipling*. London: Weidenfeld & Nicolson, 1999.

Orwell, George [pseud. of Eric Blair]. "Rudyard Kipling" (1945). In: *Kipling's Mind and Art: Selected Critical Essays*. Ed. Andrew Rutherford. Stanford, CA: Stanford University Press, 1964, p. 70-84.

Parsons, Talcott. *The Social System.* New York: Free Press, 1951.

Trompenaars, Fons/Hampden-Turner, Charles. *Building Cross-Cultural Competence: How to Create Wealth from Conflicting Values.* New Haven, CT & London: Yale University Press, 2000.

Vidal-Naquet, Pierre. *Torture: Cancer of Democracy – France and Algeria, 1954-62* [*La Torture dans la république*]. Trans. Barry Richard. Harmondsworth: Penguin, 1963.

FILM

High Noon. Dir. Fred Zinnemann, 1952.

VI.

BURNING WOMEN

Along with female circumcision, cannibalism and female infanticide, Indian widow-burning or *sati* is one of the key arguments presented by critics of cultural relativism. Surely gross acts of misogynistic cruelty can be seen as something like negative human universals, in which the appeal of basic common humanity must be allowed to outweigh the demands of a specific culture? The conservative American critic Allan Bloom in his book *The Closing of the American Mind* famously uses *sati* as a classic example of the relativistic apathy of American students. In answer to his question, "If you had been a British administrator in India, would *you* have let the natives under your governance burn the widow at the funeral of a man who had died?" they "either remain silent or reply that the British should never have been there in the first place" (Bloom, 1987, p. 26). I had a similar experience in a seminar on intercultural communication in which we discussed female circumcision and I found myself arguing against all the female students present, who insisted that, unpleasant as it was, female circumcision had to be allowed for reasons of intercultural respect. Furthermore, what right had I as a man to express strong opinions on such a subject? Wasn't my interest dirty-minded? Or just a male chauvinist attitude of moral superiority, a racist leftover from colonialism?

It was a clear demonstration to me that the discussion that has been going on in American academic circles recently, under the heading: "Is multiculturalism bad for women?", is indeed completely topical. As the journalist Katha Pollitt puts it:

> In its demand for equality for women, feminism sets itself in opposition to virtually every culture on earth. You could say that multiculturalism demands respect for all cultural traditions, while feminism interrogates and challenges all cultural traditions. [...F]unda-

mentally, the ethical claims of feminism run counter to the cultural relativism of [...] multiculturalism (Pollitt, 1999, p. 27).

Sati is therefore a sensitive subject in the debate on cultural relativism. Internationally it has been tied too closely to what is believed to be racial and colonial stereotyping for Western intellectuals to have shown much courage in speaking out against it. The most substantial Western study of *sati*, by the indologist Catherine Weinberger-Thomas (1996), skirts cautiously around questions of "for" and "against" to focus on the phenomenon of "sati-hood"; her account seems confusing and unconvincing – "distinctly shaggy and perplexing", according to one reviewer (Pinney, 2001) – almost a classic example of what happens when an anthropologist fails to translate the categories of the Other into terms meaningful to her own culture. In India, feminists are generally opposed to *sati*, but they have drawn robust censure from intellectuals like Ashis Nandy for setting up "a new form of internal colonialism" – the feminists are westernised, Anglophone city-folk rubbishing the India of the villages and small towns as backward and barbarous because they feel threatened by it (Nandy, 1994, p. 142).

Let us approach sati *from three directions – firstly, as an Indian religious and cultural phenomenon; secondly, as a Western discourse, supposedly a proof of Hindu backwardness and cruelty; and finally* sati *as it is analysed by Indian feminists.*

WHAT IS *SATI*?

"The happiest death for a woman is that which overtakes her while she is still in a wedded state," wrote the great French indologist Abbé Dubois in his *Hindu Manners, Customs and Ceremonies* (1816, p. 350), "[...] on the other hand, the greatest misfortune that can befall a wife is to survive her husband." In traditional Hindu society, widows are forbidden to wear colours, flowers, henna or turmeric decoration, or jewellery, or to eat meat. Except for lower caste or
96

Untouchable women, they are forbidden to remarry. They are expected to shave their heads, sleep on the ground, do menial work, fast, and pray for their dead husband. Among the Rajputs, in the classic *sati* area of modern India, the widow spends a year in penance, sleeping in one corner of a tiny room – "she of the corner" (*kunevali*) is an insult (Weinberger-Thomas, p. 146). Despised and helpless, and living under crowded conditions, the widow may be the object of sexual abuse within the extended family. A Marwari saying describes a young woman widowed just after her marriage: "The wedding bed just made, and she's already a whore" (*sej carhte hi rand*) (p. 147). Many widows are simply thrown out – for example, by a daughter-in-law, taking revenge for years of bullying. The choice is then often between prostitution (for younger widows) or begging.

Some are sent off to Vrindavan, Uttar Pradesh, the "city of widows" (see Dalrymple, 1998, p. 49-59; also Narasimhan, 1990, p. 54 f.), where 8,000-10,000 widows now spend their time chanting mantras to Lord Krishna (four hours of chanting for a cupful of rice and two rupees). Reportedly, the ashrams where they live are often centres of money-laundering through faked "donations". Younger widows, who may be as young as ten years old, may be sold off by the ashram managers, as concubines (sex-slaves) to local landowners or straight into brothels. In Varanasi, the holy city, there may be 20,000-60,000 widows in a similar situation, but they are less noticeable (Varanasi is a very large city, always full of pilgrims).

In the South Indian languages Kannada, Tamil and Telugu, "widow" is a term of abuse (for men, too), and a Tamil euphemism for "widow" is "she who is no longer alive" (Narasimhan, p. 40); in some northern languages, the words for "widow" and "prostitute" are either very similar or identical, and "widow" (*rand*) is a term of abuse (Jamanadas, *Devadasis*). In May 2000 the National Human Rights Commission of India requested provincial governments to ban the word "widow" in official records as derogatory, and a year later the government of Jammu and Kashmir prohibited use of the Hindi and Urdu words (Hussain, 2001).

An attempt by the Indian director Deepa Mehta to make a film about the plight of widows in India was abandoned after violent protests from Hindu religious leaders, although at the time of writing (September 2004) a controversial new film on the subject, *White Rainbows*, by an Indian-American director, Dharan Mandrayar, is about to hit Indian cinemas (Anand, 2004).

In earlier times it was often said that the plight of a widow was so unpleasant that the brief agony of *sati* was better than the long agony of widowhood. In the words of a British observer at the height of the Raj, "The wretched condition forced on widows by national custom causes many of them to prefer being burnt on the pile with their dead husbands" (Eden, 1876, p. 120 f.).

Widow-burning can be found in many historical cultures, along with the immolation of a ruler's or a nobleman's slaves, horses and favourite objects. It has existed in India since at least 510 A.D. (Thapar, 1966, p. 152), although there are earlier references in religious texts, probably to a symbolic enactment, and in the account of India in the late fourth century B.C. by Megasthenes, ambassador of the Greek king Seleucus Nicator (Rawlinson, 1925, p. 59), where it is a curiosity practised only among certain tribes.

In more modern times, *sati* has been particularly associated with the warlike Rajputs of what is now Rajasthan, an area roughly the same size as modern Germany, whose womenfolk had a tradition, *jauhar*, of mass suicide in defeat. At the end of a battle a flag would be raised to signal victory or defeat, and if it was the latter, the women would kill themselves. The most famous, albeit possibly mythical, story concerns the mass suttee of Queen Padmini and her women at Chittor, to avoid capture by the Muslim Sultan of Delhi, Ala-ud-din Khilji, in 1303 (Weinberger-Thomas, p. 122). Later, during the sixteenth century, there were further large-scale acts of *jauhar* at Chittor, reportedly involving vast numbers of women. Widow-burning was common among the princes and the higher castes. Sixty-six women were burnt at the funeral of Ajit Singh of Marwar (Jodhpur) in 1724, and eighty-four died at the funeral of Budh Singh, Rajah of Bundi (Narasimhan, p. 119). It is easy to see a connection between *jau-*

har and *sati*, at least in the sense that the Rajput custom made the Rajputs favourably inclined towards *sati* – and perhaps there *is* a homology here, but *jauhar* is something that took place in a military rather than religious context.

The Muslim rulers of India – the Sultans of Delhi, and later the Mughal emperors – discouraged *sati*, but they didn't forbid it, for fear of causing rebellion among their Hindu subjects. They were not being soft-hearted (bear in mind that traitors or convicted criminals might be impaled, skinned alive or crushed by an elephant), however, Hindu widows were seen as innocent victims of an irrational heathen religion. Although *sati* was seen as suicide, which was forbidden by *Sharia* law, it was permitted to Hindu widows provided that it genuinely *was* voluntary (Thapar, p. 292). Akbar (1556-1605), the greatest of the Mughals, "took personal pains to see that no compulsion should be used" (Lane-Poole, 1903, p. 253), and reportedly rode a hundred miles in an attempt to prevent the *sati* of a Rajput princess (Narasimhan, p. 109).

The attitude of the British during the early years of East India Company rule was very similar, and they only took steps against *sati* when they realised that they would not be opposed by the Hindu community. In contrast, the Portuguese administration in Goa forbade *sati* as early as 1510 (*ibid.*). The richest part of British India was Bengal, and the Bengali city of Calcutta was the capital of British India and the residence of the British governor-general. The Bengali intellectual and reformer Ram Mohan Roy, who had seen his own widowed sister-in-law burnt in 1812 – "an hysterical and unhappy sacrifice" (quoted in Allan *et al.*, 1934, p. 722) – without being able to help her, led a campaign against *sati* in print and also by trying to stop actual burnings in Calcutta (there was an average of one a day). He suggested that *sati* in Bengal was often motivated by the greed of the dead man's family, since under the inheritance law prevalent in Bengal, *dayabhaga*, widows inherited the whole estate of the dead husband and could not sell or mortgage it or even give it away (Narasimhan, p. 115 f.). Roy's efforts strengthened the resolve of reformers in the BEIC to do something about *sati*. Previously they had tended to follow a "hands off" policy, in

99

order to avoid offending Hindu sensibilities. A regulation in 1812, for example, announced that *sati* was permitted if voluntary – many widows have been brought to the pyre sedated with opium or other drugs – and if the widow was not under 16 and not pregnant (Moon, 1989, p. 457).

The presence of a police officer to enforce these details effectively gave *sati* official sanction in the eyes of the local population, a rather unfortunate effect, and in Bengal the number of cases of *sati* increased drastically, although a cholera epidemic might also have been responsible, in the sense that there were suddenly a lot more widows (Narasimhan, p. 68). In 1829, however, the British governor-general Lord William Bentinck banned it. Under Regulation XVII, *sati* was declared to be either culpable homicide, punishable with imprisonment, or murder, punishable with death. Bentinck was clever enough to consult opinion among the sepoys – the Indian soldiers – first, and he found that they were fairly indifferent – they came mostly from areas where *sati* was uncommon (Moon, p. 456). He also consulted Sanskrit scholars, police inspectors, local administrators, and Ram Mohan Roy. Not all Indians were opposed to *sati*. Roy himself was not actually in favour of a direct ban (Embree, 1994, p. 153 f.). Many Indians saw the *sati* – the burning widow – as an important national symbol, the epitomy of self-sacrifice and of moral and spiritual energy.

This attitude is still surprisingly prevalent today. A quick tour through Indian web sites and discussion forums soon reveals people willing to glorify the *sati* or anxious to repeal or modify anti-*sati* legislation. *Sati*, like female infanticide and human sacrifice (see Karmakar, 2002, on the attempts to revive human sacrifice in Assam), has never completely died out in India. Today the centre of *sati* is Rajasthan, the land of the Rajputs, in particular the semi-desert area called Marwar ("the region of death"), where there are cult centres of Sati Mata ("Mother Suttee"). Those who burn themselves bring good fortune to their families and villages for seven generations. In country areas you see little *sati* cenotaphs, or *chattris*; in forts or palaces, the *nishan* (mark) of a hand on a stone tablet or painted on the wall commemorates a *sati* (traditionally, a *sati* would make the mark in henna just before mounting the pyre).

In the past half century since Independence there have been at least forty cases of *sati* in rural areas (Weinberger-Thomas, p. 182 f.), three-quarters of them in Rajasthan and most of these in the district of Sikar near Jaipur, though possibly many more unpublicised cases. The number will now need to be increased by one more since the burning of sixty-five-year-old Kuttu Bai in a village in Madhya Pradesh on August 6, 2002 (Anonymous, 2002). The most notorious *sati* was the burning of eighteen-year-old Roop Kanwar in Deorala on September 4, 1987, for which thirty-seven men were put on trial and (after nine years) acquitted. The account of the Deorala case given here is based largely on Narasimhan (1990) and the relevant sections of Hawley (Ed., 1994).

Roop Kanwar was well-educated, her father ran a trucking company in Jaipur, the state capital, her husband Mal Singh – who died suddenly under mysterious circumstances, quite possibly suicide – was a science graduate and the son of a village schoolteacher who himself had bachelor's and master's degrees. Deorala is a prosperous village of 10,000 with electricity and tap-water, a hospital, two secondary schools, and a literacy rate of 70%.

The court case polarised India. Westernised urban-dwellers believed the version of murder by a primitive mob; villagers believed that Roop Kunwar had made a glorious choice. Within two weeks of her death, three-quarters of a million people had come to worship at the site of her *sati*. 250,000-300,000 alone attended the "glorification" ceremony, or "Festival of the Veil" (*chunari mahotsav*) thirteen days after the event, at which the embers were doused with Ganges water and milk, and the crowd included state politicians and state MPs. When Rajiv Gandhi's federal government made it illegal to glorify *sati*, a crowd of 70,000 demonstrated in Jaipur against this. A poll in *The Times of India* in December 1987 showed 63.4% support for *sati*.

Religious leaders like the Shankaracharya of Puri – the abbot of one of the four most famous Hindu monasteries, there is no Hindu pope, but his Christian equivalent would be someone like a cardinal or archbishop – spoke out strongly against the new legislation, saying that *sati* was a recognised part of Hindu tradition and supported by scripture.

Actually, the Hindu scriptures are ambiguous on this subject. The earliest holy texts, the Vedas, contain references to widows remarrying, but no direct mention of self-immolation, except possibly one very controversial section of the *Rig-Veda* X, 18, 7 f. (c.1300 B.C. or later) which seems to describe the widow stepping forward to lie down beside the body on the pyre before being called back to the land of the living. This could be a ritual gesture of paying last respects; or a symbolic rejection of a yet earlier tradition of immolation; but in some versions it may also be a corrupt text, with the verb -*agne*, to "go into the fire" (from *agni*, fire), substituted for -*agre*, to "come forward". The result is an unclear reading, perhaps the result of a transcription mistake by a scribe or, in the view of the famous indologist Max Müller, a deliberate later corruption of the text by unscrupulous priests (Narasimhan, p. 14). The later *Atharva-Veda* XVIII, 2, 1 contains an appeal to a widow to get up from beside her husband's body and offers a prayer for her future life with wealth and children (*ibid.*). Kautilya's *Arthashastra* (300 B.C. or later) mentions widow remarriage; the *Laws of Manu* (second century B.C.-second century A.D.?), the basis of later Hindu lawgiving, do not mention *sati* at all (*ibid.*). The references to *sati* come in later works, and, as Narasimhan points out (*op. cit.*, p. 18), what can be observed is a process reflecting a chronological shift in attitudes to women (and not at all to their advantage) by which, first, remarriage of widows is allowed; then, celibacy is encouraged; then, celibacy and *sati* are suggested as alternatives; then, *sati* is encouraged; and, finally, in texts after about 700 A.D., there is glorification of *sati*.

The logic of *sati* – the word properly refers not to the act but to the person carrying it out – is one of female devotion. *Sat* is "essence/inner truth/goodness/purity" – the good wife (*sati*) is true to her ideals of chastity, purity and loyalty to her husband, is a *pativrata*, who has made a vow (*vrat*) to her lord husband (*pati*), who sees him as husband-as-god (*patidev*) and joins him in death. If a woman is completely devoted to her husband, she will die first. If he dies before her, she has failed him in some way. However, she can re-store the situation by vowing to join him in death (*sativrata*). She is full of the moral heat of *sat*, and will ignite spontaneously and explosively on the funeral pyre. From now on until her death she is in a kind of mystic state, able to make terrible curses and utter commands that must be obeyed. In death she becomes *satimata*, a goddess who will protect her family from beyond the grave.

Not all Hindu groups indulged in *sati*, and *sati* was never a general obligation. In his account of India in the late thirteenth century, Marco Polo mentions *sati* (for which women can earn great praise) (Polo, The Yule Edition, p.258), but also several cases of widowed queens, such as the ruling queen of Mutfili (p. 265) or the widowed mother of the five kings of Maabar (p. 271). In the tantric tradition, which venerates the Mother Goddess, *sati* is absolutely taboo and women who become *sati* – and men who help them to – go straight to hell (Oldenburg, 1994a, p. 171). *Sati* has also been very rare among the Jains, possibly because Jain widows are allowed to become nuns (Narasimhan, p. 43).

Even those Hindu texts that encourage *sati* usually forbid it for Brahmin women. Possibly the priests were trying to protect their own womenfolk (p. 20), but the more likely explanation is that *sati* was a custom of the warrior castes, the *kshatriya*, who were concerned about the damage to their personal honour threatened by the violation of their women, especially defenceless widows, in a period of violence and confusion, the so-called Indian Middle Ages, that followed the collapse of the Gupta Empire in the fifth century AD, the invasions of the Huns and the brief empire of Harsha (605-647). (This is roughly the period in which positive references to *sati* begin to predominate.) Rajasthan was India's Wild West, the war front with invaders like the Huns and the Muslims.

THE WESTERN DISCOURSE OF *SATI*

From the Western point of view, *sati* has not always been merely a theoretical problem – the British ruled India for two hundred years, and had to decide what, if anything, to do about it. But *sati* was well-known in the West long before the British colonial period. Almost every traveller's account of India included a description – and often a picture – of *sati*.

In 1441 the Italian merchant Nicolò de' Conti reported what he had seen on his travels in India (Lach, 1965, p. 61 f.). In 1502, an Indian Christian priest, Joseph, travelled to Rome and told Pope Alexander VI about such customs as *sati* (p. 157). The Venetian merchant Cesare de Fedrici gave a detailed account of *sati* after staying in Vijayanagar in southern India for seven months in 1567 – he had lived near the gate through which the *sati* processions left the city (p.471). The Dutchman Jan van Linschoten left a similar account about twenty years later, and both he and Fedrici repeat the explanation of *sati* that once upon a time wives had been so apt to get rid of their husbands by poison that the law had to be introduced which compelled a widow to be burnt with her dead husband (p. 485), a tale originally told by the Greek Diodorus Siculus, and quoted by Gandhi (Narasimhan, p. 57).

Westerners were fascinated by *sati*, and the accounts were turned to different uses in Europe. As Figueira (1994) has shown, European writers used *sati* as a means to criticise brutal, irrational religion (Voltaire, Herder), or to speculate about reincarnation, or as an expression of overwhelming love-in-death, *e.g.*, Goethe's *Der Gott und die Bajadere* (1797), in which the woman burns herself on the dead god's pyre, and he returns and lifts her up into heaven. In non-Indian form it appears in Brünnhilde's self-immolation in Wagner's *Götterdämmerung* (1876), and perhaps also in Miss Havisham's in Dickens's *Great Expectations* (1861). But the British colonial accounts are normally on a different level, of practical and personal involvement, and they need to be considered in the functional context of a handful of British wielding power over one hundred million Indians.

Sati was a touchstone of native inferiority, and an excuse for British interference. Social horrors like *sati* were useful reminders to the Indians of the need for benevolent, civilising British rule – especially at times of vocal nationalism, like the 1920s, which saw the publication of books like Edward Thompson's "historical" study *Suttee* (1928) and

Katherine Mayo's aggressive *Mother India* (1927) and *Slaves of the Gods* (1929). The central figure in British accounts is usually the male British protagonist who is drawn into a social drama and confronted with the need to respond emotionally and perhaps practically. The *sati* rescue was a theatrical opportunity for the Western male to demonstrate racial and moral superiority – the colonies as a stage for the kind of self-dramatisation that was much less easily achievable in Europe. It was an enactment of power that was both racist and sexist – as Gayatri Chakravorty Spivak memorably if somewhat glibly puts it, "white men saving brown women from brown men" (Spivak, 1988, p. 297; see also Jarman, 1998, p. 86 f.).

Even before the banning of *sati*, there was considerable leeway for local (British) authorities to intervene to prevent it. Some magistrates or officers would declare that they would permit the *sati* if the widow burnt her finger first – which might put a stop to the project (Narasimhan, p. 66), or might not (Weinberger-Thomas, p. 41-43). This is somewhat reminiscent of Voltaire's *Zadig* (1747), in which Zadig suggests introducing a law "par laquelle il ne serait permis à une veuve de se brûler qu'après avoir entretenu un jeune homme en tête à tête pendant une heure entière" (chapitre XI, *le Bûcher*), *i.e.*, a law to make widows spend an hour alone with a young man before they are allowed to sacrifice themselves.

Sir Charles Napier, conqueror of Sind, when told by local Brahmins that *sati* was an established tradition, replied that hanging people who burnt women was an established tradition among the British, and that both sides should therefore follow their traditions (actually, there was very little *sati* in Sind, which was predominantly Muslim) (Moon, p. 577). One magistrate saved a woman who had leapt from the flames into the Ganges from being forcibly burnt by the mob by telling them that since the sacred river had rejected the woman's sacrifice – the non-swimmer had not drowned (she was in fact rescued by a police boat) – then they should not intervene (Narasimhan, p. 96); more recently (1985) a brave Indian police officer saved a *sati* from being burnt in front of a crowd of 20,000 by telling the participants in the ritual to wait for her to ignite spontaneously – after an hour, when it was clear that she was not a "true *sati*", he was able to send everyone home (p. 96 f.).

In fairness to some of the *sati* rescuers, though it may well be that they acted for ethnocentric or hegemonistic reasons, surely there was also an element of compassion on the simple level of one human being to another, an emotional rather than a moral imperative. It need not have excluded erotic interest – human motivation, to my mind, is seldom straightforward. The proof of this would lie in the willingness of the rescuer to accept the consequences of his action, perhaps risking his life, or his job, or taking responsibility for the person into whose life he had intruded.

Thus Job Charnock, the later founder of Calcutta, and reputedly not a particularly pleasant man, rescued a beautiful fifteen-year-old widow, a Rajput princess, from the pyre in Bihar (c.1663) and then married her himself; they had several daughters, who married into English families of substance, and he mourned her by sacrificing a cockerel in her honour every year on the day of her death, a gesture – in the view of his contemporaries – of "unusual though innocent excess" (Moorhouse, 1971, p. 29; Wilkinson, 1976, p. 30). Today, we are all expected to be cultural relativists – a position that is itself culturally determined rather than universal – and if you are going to say "No! Stop it!" to another culture, then it is far better for it to be for personal reasons rather than in the name of your own "superior" one.

Some modern commentators – for example Lata Mani (1998) – have approached the subject of *sati* as if it only existed as a British discursive construct. The British set the agenda by claiming that Indians were deterministically enslaved by religion, and that *sati* was religiously based. They supposedly gave structure and recognition to the custom by consulting only the spokesmen of the Hindu elite, and then following their recommendations. They exaggerated the significance of a regional, caste-restricted phenomenon, and distinguished between "good" *satis* that were voluntary, spiritual and noble, and "bad" *satis* that were coercive and engineered by greedy priests and relatives. The fate of the unfortunate woman burned to death was of little concern.

The approach adopted here smacks of self-deluding political correctness. The discursive manipulation of *sati* by Westerners need not exclude the fact that *sati* as a ceremony (and not the self-immolation of religious or political fanatics that you find in many cultures) was a well-established Indian tradition, reported on by visitors to India for two thousand years; that it took place in a religious context; and that it was homologous with the abuse and exploitation of women that was (and still is) characteristic of traditional Indian society. To state, as Lata Mani does, that "The discussion of the rights of women as individuals is [...] strikingly absent in the debate" (p. 77) may be true, but it is a rather strange, historicist thing to say – has she forgotten what conditions for women were like in Europe in, say, 1820?

In any case, having got themselves into the colonial situation, what were the British to do? If they interfered in *sati*, then it was ethnocentric meddling and racist assertion of superiority. If they didn't, it was opportunistic toleration of the oppression of women in the name of a religious tradition that they didn't properly understand. This is a "no-win situation".

It also seems questionable to ascribe a monolithic response to the British. There were different reactions, just as there were different agendas. Some British reactions were callous, along the lines of "Let them get on with it!" Sati could also be the object of sick humour, as in the mid-nineteenth century cigarette advertising slogan "With only a Suttee's passion / To do their duty and burn" (quoted in Harlow/Carter, 1999, p. 68). Local administrators, as already indicated, were often left alone with their instincts and consciences to decide whether to intervene or not.

Thomas Twining (1792, in Kaul, 1979) found himself in such a situation. As the *sati* circles the pyre, Twining talks to her, trying unsuccessfully to dissuade her and offering her financial inducements. He is aware of "the pressure of the Bramins [*sic*], watchful lest their victim should escape, obliging her to move on" (p. 94). On her last round of the pyre, Twining talks to her again and senses (or thinks that he senses) her reluctance: "[…] her countenance impressed me with the assurance that if she had been free from the fatal influence which surrounded her it would not have been difficult to turn her from her resolution" (*ibid.*). He notes the enthusiasm of the bystanders, but sees no sign of either horror or pity on their faces.

Accounts, including fictional ones, were bound to focus on the British official, whether an anguished, helpless observer or a bold rescuer, if only because the (potentially) dynamic is usually more interesting dramaturgically than the merely acted upon. But there is variation in the way in which *sati* is portrayed. For example, some eighteenth-century pictures emphasise the dignified, noble aspect of *sati*, with the figures looking almost Classical in their robes; this is still true of the tableau by Captain Grindlay published in 1844 (*Illustration 4*) – after dreaming of the death of her husband, the woman burned herself near Baroda, in the princely state of Gwalior, after resisting the persuasions of both the British Resident, Sir James Rivett Carnac, and the local prince, Daulat Rao Scindia (see Weinberger-Thomas, p.103).

It is not true of such drawings that they "neglect" the victim. In the early nineteenth century the British East India Company came under attack, for example from missionaries (who had been largely excluded from India), as compromising itself morally for commercial gain. The pictures in missionary pamphlets tend to be naive or melodramatic, but they are *involved*, with villainous Indians waving swords (highly unlikely at a burning) or with distraught European observers turning away from the horror.

Illustration 4 (opposite page): "A Suttee – Preparing for the Immolation of a Hindoo Widow," a steel engraving by J. Redaway from a drawing by Captain Grindlay, Fisher, Son, & Co., 1844.

The classic fictional account of a *sati* rescue is not British, but French – the account of the rescuing of Aouda in Jules Verne's *Around the World in 80 Days* (*Le Tour du monde en quatre-vingt jours*, 1873) – and at least certain elements of it are ironical. A few interesting points stand out:

- that Aouda's immolation is connected with the cult of Kali, "perhaps the most terrifying of all the manifestations of the Great Goddess" (Blurton, 1992, p. 172), a Hindu deity of frightening appearance and sinister reputation, whose cult has traditionally been associated with death, blood sacrifice and ritual murder. Her name means the "Black (female) One". However, *sati* and Kali have scarcely any connection with each other, and this is more a case of two Indian "horrors" being linked with each other automatically;

- that Aouda, who later marries the hero Phileas Fogg, is pale-skinned (Chapter 12: "blanche comme une Européenne"). Much Western fantasising about exotic sex has played safe by making the non-European woman look or actually turn out to be white; in the case of films, she is often played by a white actress, as Aouda is played by Shirley MacLaine in the film *Around the World in 80 Days* (1956);

- that the central figure in the rescue is the white man. That is normal enough, but in this instance, ironically, the rescuer is Phileas Fogg's French servant Passepartout – this is after all a novel by a Frenchman!;

- and that Aouda shows deep gratitude towards and admiration for her "rescuer".

The two best-known modern fictional accounts of *sati* are both untypical. *The Deceivers* (1952) by John Masters, who was an officer in the British Army in India before becoming a bestselling novelist, is about *thagi* (thuggee), ritual murder in honour of Kali, another Indian custom that the British tried to eradicate, but there is an important plot element involving *sati*. At the beginning of the story the hero, William Savage, saves a widow from burning herself by means of a trick. The description of *sati* – voluntary *sati*, that is – is suprisingly understanding. At the end of the novel Savage, who has lived as an Indian in disguise, helps the

110

woman to become a *sati* by lighting the fire for her himself. (She also dies at the end of the film version directed by Nicholas Meyer, 1988, but he doesn't himself light the pyre.)

M. M. Kaye's *The Far Pavilions* (1978) was a huge bestseller. There is a *sati* scene, but it is not the heroine, Anjuli, who is to die but her spoilt, cruel sister Shushila. In the rather overwrought plot, Shushila wishes to exclude her sister from the honour of *sati* and from sharing the funeral pyre of their dead husband; she is to watch, and afterwards her eyes will be put out (in the television version, directed by Peter Duffell, 1983, this is on Shushila's orders, but in the book she is not quite so sadistic). Anjuli is rescued by her lover Ash, who agrees to shoot Shushila on the funeral pyre so that she will not feel the pain of burning.

THE FEMINIST PERSPECTIVE

It is easy to make a case that South Asian society is male chauvinistic. The treatment of widows seems to be part of a nexus of female inferiority, expendability and abuse that also includes infanticide; child-brides; wife-beating; the rape of low-caste women or (in Pakistan) members of the Christian minority; honour killings, known as *karo kari* in rural Pakistan (Griffin, 1996); dowry murders; and temple prostitution. Narasimhan quotes the ancient texts at length to support this view:

> A man with a hundred tongues would die before finishing the task of lecturing upon the vices and defects of women, even if he were to do nothing else throughout a long life of a hundred years (*Mahabharata*, c.400 B.C.-A.D. 200, quoted in Narasimhan, p. 28).

"Women, low-castes, dogs and crows embody untruth, sin and darkness", they "have the hearts of hyenas" says another text (*Satapatha Brahmana*) (p. 29); and there is a proverb: "The drum, the village fool, the low-caste, animals and women – all these are fit to be beaten" (p. 51). The Laws of Manu declare that in childhood a woman should be in the

111

charge of her father, in youth of her husband, and in old age of her son (p. 31). A woman's life only has meaning in the context of a man's, and a woman should be "used" only by one man – one nineteenth-century religious commentator, Pandit Ghanashyamji of Bombay, even compared women with "one-way" crockery (p. 34) – so celibacy or suttee become logical. There was (is?) a fear of female sexuality – Hindu society, all those erotic temple carvings and sexy mythological stories notwithstanding, is extremely prudish. Ram Mohan Roy pointed out to the British how worried many Indian families were that a widow might "go astray" – *sati* removed that fear for them (p. 33).

Modern Indian society does not encourage equality between the sexes. At the centre of the problem is the phenomenon of dowry. On visits to India in the 1970s and 1980s, I noticed a strong difference to usual Indian practices when I spent time in villages of the "tribal" Bhils of Rajasthan and Madhya Pradesh. The Bhils had a bride-price rather than a dowry system – the bridegroom "bought" his bride, and if she was unhappy she could return to her parents without any obligation on them to return his money. I observed how often women seemed to have the say in public situations, and was told that the Bhils attached no great importance to premarital virginity – it was accepted that older children would experiment with each other sexually – although a non-virgin tended to command a lower bride-price.

The dowry system on the other hand has encouraged the custom of female infanticide. In 1991, there were 945 girls for every 1,000 boys, in 2001 only 927 (Wadhwa, 2002). Female infanticide is especially prevalent in the south of India – with Tamil Nadu, where the problem hit the headlines in 1986, supposedly having the greatest incidence (Sen, 2001, p. 78). It was calculated by the Community Services Guild of Tamil Nadu that in the areas they were studying around 44% of the female children born in 1991 had been murdered (Anonymous, *Gender equity and justice*). As in many other Asian countries, sons are more highly valued because of their greater physical strength, their role in the family cult – in India, the lighting of the funeral pyre – and because they remain within the family after marriage rather

112

than leaving it (the years of upbringing are therefore a better investment than with girls). But a major reason for the killing of newborn baby girls, perhaps the most important, is the huge burden of later having to provide a dowry for them.

The repertoire of baby murder covers a whole range of killing techniques (Wadhwa, 1995; Venkatesan, 2001), including strangling, snapping the spine, filling the baby's mouth with tobacco juice, fertiliser or black salt, feeding it hot, spicy chicken soup, poisoning with oleander, leaving the umbilical cord untied, suffocating the baby in a clay pot, or (a method I myself encountered in Calcutta in the 1980s) leaving the baby on a rubbish dump, to be eaten by dogs. But it is not only female *children* who are done away with.

There is also the phenomenon of dowry murder. In Delhi alone, there is a murder or attempted murder of a young wife, usually by her mother-in-law, at the rate of more than one a day, the motive being greed for yet another dowry payment. (Dowry was abolished by law in 1961, but is still overwhelmingly prevalent.) At Delhi's Tihar Jail, a separate barrack for murderous mothers-in-law has had to be built, and is already overcrowded (Anonymous, 2000). These murders are usually by burning, and are often disguised as kitchen accidents or cases of suicide. They became noticeable in the early 1970s in northern India, and are apparently particularly common among the Marwaris (Weinberger-Thomas, p. 165). There are indications that they are beginning to spread to the Asian communities in Britain, where the suicide rate among young South Asian women is suspiciously high (Prentice, 2000). Not all Indians are as outraged about these attacks as Indian feminists are. Women who survive these attacks may be ostracised, after all, if the woman was abused or abandoned by her husband, she must somehow have provoked it, have been to blame by not being a good wife (Sen, p. 67) .

A few Indian feminists have adopted a more traditional, universalist position, questioning the emphasis on dowry as a motive and seeing these killings as examples of male chauvinist hatred and domestic violence, or have focused on inheritance laws rather than dowry as the root of the problem. Overstressing dowry creates an erroneous impression that all of the violence in Indian homes is due to a growing greed for more dowry. And it makes the crime look peculiarly Indian, while the truth is that violence against wives is common to most societies, including those which have no tradition of dowry (Kishwar 2001; but see also Agnes, 2002, and the discussion in Sen, p. 181 f.).

Ironically, there has probably been less interest among Westerners in these very numerous dowry murders by burning than there has been about the tiny handful of *sati* cases. Is it because we can "accept" greed as a motive for killing far more easily than we can accept religious enthusiasm? The American indologist Ainslie Embree (1994) has suggested that the truly horrific and disturbing thing about Deorala was that many thousands celebrated it, and claimed religious sanction for it. This is a dichotomous culture in which, parallel to the abuses to which women are subjected, the different forms of the Mother Goddess are worshipped with tremendous enthusiasm. Indian defenders of *sati* will say that it glorifies the widow into a goddess, that it is an affirmation of female strength and power. *Sati* is an opportunity, if voluntary, for women to fulfil themselves magnificently in a society where (admittedly) such role opportunities are very few. It is an Indian (Hindu) way, which makes sense within the logic of traditional Indian (Hindu) culture and cannot be understood and should not be criticised by non-Indians.

This might seem a seductive argument in the Indian context, and even of appeal to cultural relativists with a guilty conscience about the arrogance of colonialism, but it has been undermined by criticisms not merely by culturally chauvinistic Westerners but from within India as well.

For example, it is possible to analyse what occurred in Deorala in sober socio-economic terms. In the view of the feminist groups who led the protests against *sati* at state and national level, what happened to Roop Kanwar is very like what happened to another young widow, Om Kanwar, in 1980. Om Kanwar was murdered, and her killing disguised as a *sati* to the advantage of the three most powerful groups

114

in Rajasthan, namely the traditional Rajputs, no longer a great military and landowning force, and in need of the ideological boost to their status of a well-publicised suttee; the Brahmin priests, who would gain in prestige and wealth by their administration of a holy event; and the Marwari merchants – an unholy alliance of feudal chauvinism, religion and money (see Oldenburg, 1994). After all, *sati* is big business. The immediate family, local shopkeepers and transport companies can make huge profits out of the crowds coming to visit the *sati* site, or *sati sthal*, selling them refreshments, incense and coconuts as offerings, and commemorative items like photographs. An annual fair may be started. If a temple is erected, huge sums may be collected in offerings. In Deorala they reportedly collected more than seven million rupees (Narasimhan, p. 134). The site of Om Kanwar's *sati* is also a popular pilgrimage site.

Among the keenest supporters of *sati* are the Marwari businessmen and bankers whose families spread out from Rajasthan and who now control much of the Indian economy. Wealthy, but backward and superstitious, they are themselves middle-caste (*vaisya*), but tend to identify enviously with the warlike Rajput traditions. It happens that in the area from which most of them originate, Shekhavati, there is a town, Jhunjhunu, which is a famous *satimata* cult centre. A *sati* gives them the chance to network with their rural place of origin, make themselves important and make money. "Small desert townships, economically ravaged by several years of drought, sprout gaudy shrines and become booming pilgrim sites; impoverished petty Rajput families win god, gold, and glory by murdering their teen-aged widowed daughters-in-law; local politicians win another election" (Oldenburg, 1994a, p. 161).

There may have been more personal motives at work, too. Roop Kunwar's in-laws stood to lose a lot of money if she had returned, with her dowry, to her own parents – which is apparently the local tradition in the case of young widows without children. Her dowry had been very substantial, consisting of about $8,400 in gold, hundreds of dollars in other payments, a colour television, a kitchen stove, a refrigerator, furniture, clothes and gifts. Roop Kanwar's parents were not informed until after her death, something which seems to have happened in all the recent *sati* cases in that part of Rajasthan. Normally, when a young man dies his in-laws will be informed immediately, and the Kanwars were only two hours away by car, but their presence at the cremation would have made it more difficult to carry out a *sati*. Even so, they caused no trouble afterwards, and even contributed 100,000 rupees towards the celebration of the first anniversary of the *sati* (Oldenburg, 1994, p. 119).

Finally, the question needs to be asked: what, in a traditional Indian context, does "voluntary" actually mean? Given the nature of the pressures on Indian women in traditional rural areas, given that they have little part in the choice of education, career, or husband, and that they have their lives determined for them throughout by men, is it reasonable to talk in terms of free choice and coercion? Far from being wholly a modern perception, this is the conclusion that was reached in 1818 by Walter Ewer, who was Acting Superintendent of Police in the Lower Provinces (Weinberger-Thomas, p. 109 f.). More recently, in the words of a report by the three women sent by the Women and Media Committee of the Bombay Union of Journalists to find out what had happened in Deorala (they concluded that Roop Kanwar had been murdered): "A choice can be made only between viable alternatives, for many women, there are no alternatives" (Sen, p. 30).

Soma Wadhwa (1996) has described how, during a great festival at the *sati* temple in Jhunjhunu, a slightly confused French tourist caused tremendous shock by asking whether women in India who wanted to commit *sati* had to come to this temple to do so. One of the worshippers told him: "India is a progressive country. Women are not burnt here. They are respected. To us they are mothers, devis, goddesses. We worship them." Soma Wadwha's comment was: "Do women want to be worshipped? Or, would they rather have equal rights?"

Whatever difficulties may arise in the intercultural encounter, the truly unforgivable act of cultural arrogance is not that of the critic of such customs as *sati*, provided that the criticisms are honest, humane, context-sensitive, and ex-

116

plicatory in intention; it is the laziness of the knee-jerk relativist, who, paying homage to political correctness, substitutes indifference for involvement, and mistakes "tolerance" for understanding.

REFERENCES

Agnes, Flavia (2002). "Chilling Narratives." In: *The Hindu Literary Review, online edition.* Web page, April 7, 2002, <http://www.hinduonnet.com/thehindu/lr/2002/04/07/stories/2002040700240500.htm> (Accessed: 30.08.2004)

Allan, J./Haig, T. W./Dodwell, H. H. *The Cambridge Shorter History of India.* Cambridge: Cambridge University Press, 1934.

Anand, Anu (2004). "Film Highlight's [*sic*] Widows' Plight." In: *BBC News, world edition.* Web page, <http://news.bbc.co.uk/2/hi/south_asia/3611848.stm> (10.09.2004)

Anonymous (*Gender equity and justice*). "Gender Equity and Justice." In: *National Foundation for India.* Web page, <http://nfidel.tripod.com/gender.html> (30.08.2004)

— (2000)."Mother-in-Law Cells in Tihar." In: *Net-GuruIndia – Headlines.* Web page, May 2000, <http://www.calonline.com/news/may00/del23may00.html#r2>(Accessed: 30.08.2004)

— (2002). "Outrage over India Ritual Burning." In: *BBC News, world edition.* Web page, <http://news.bbc.co.uk/2/hi/south_asia/2180380.stm> (30.08.2004)

Bloom, Allan. *The Closing of the American Mind.* New York: Simon & Schuster, 1987.

Blurton, T. Richard. *Hindu Art.* London: British Museum Press, 1992.

Dalrymple, William (1998). *The Age of Kali: Indian Travels & Encounters.* London: Flamingo, 1999.

Dickens, Charles (1861). *Great Expectations.* London/New York: Dent/Dutton, 1962.

Dubois, Abbé J. A. (1816). *Hindu Manners, Customs and Ceremonies* [*Moeurs, institutions et cérémonies des peuples de l'Inde*] (first English edition, 1816). Trans. Henry

K. Beauchamp. New Delhi & Madras: Asian Educational Services, 1983.

Eden, Charles H. *India – Historical and Descriptive.* London: Marcus Ward & Co., 1876.

Embree, Ainslee T. (1994). "Comment: Widows as Cultural Symbols." In: Hawley (Ed.), p. 149-59.

Figueira, Dorothy (1994). "Die Flambierte Frau: Sati in European Culture." In: Hawley (Ed.), p. 55-72.

Goethe, J. W. (1797). "Der Gott und die Bajadere." In: *Sämtliche Werke nach Epochen seines Schreibens (Münchner Ausgabe), Band 4.1.* Ed. Reiner Wild. Munich: Carl Hanser, 1988, p. 872-74.

Griffin, Jennifer. "Women Murdered by Tradition." In: *The Observer,* January 28, 1996, p. 19.

Harlow, Barbara/Carter, M. (Eds.). *Imperialism & Orientalism: A Documentary Sourcebook.* Oxford: Blackwell, 1999.

Hawley, John Stratton (Ed.). *Sati, the Blessing and the Curse: The Burning of Wives in India.* New York & Oxford: Oxford University Press, 1994.

Hussain, Altaf (2001). "Kashmir Bans the Widow Word." In: *BBC News, world edition.* Web page, <http://news.bbc.co.uk/2/hi/south_asia/1459292.stm> (10.09.2004)

Jamanadas, Dr. K. (*Devadasis*). "Devadasis Were Degraded Buddhist Nuns." In: *Dalit E-Forum.* Web page, <http://www.ambedkar.org/buddhism/Devadasis_Were_Deg raded_Buddhist_Nuns.htm> (30.08.2004)

Jarman, Francis. *The Perception of Asia: Japan and the West.* Hildesheim: Hildesheim University Press, 1998.

Karmakar, Rahul (2002): "Indian Temple Revives 'Human Sacrifice'". In: *BBC News, world edition.* Web page, <http://news.bbc.co.uk/2/hi/south_asia/1908706.stm> (30.08. 2004)

Kaul, H. K. (Ed.) (1979). *Travellers' India: An Anthology.* Delhi: Oxford University Press, 1997.

Kautilya (300 B.C. or later). *Arthashastra.* In: *Indian History Sourcebook.* Web page, <http://www.fordham.edu/halsall/india/kautilya1.html#Book%20III,%20Chapter%202> (30.08.2004)

Kaye, M. M. *The Far Pavilions*. Harmondsworth: Allen Lane, 1978.

Kishwar, Madhu (2001). "India's New Abuse Laws Still Miss the Mark." From *Manushi*, reprinted in *Hinduism Today*. Web page, Sept./Oct. 2001, <http://www.hinduismtoday.com/2001/9-10/44-47dowry.html> (30.08.2004)

Lach, Donald F. *Asia in the Making of Europe. Volume I: The Century of Discovery, Book One*. Chicago & London: Chicago University Press, 1965.

Lane-Poole, Stanley (1903). *Mediaeval India under Mohammedan Rule (A.D. 712-1764)*. Delhi: Low Price Publications, 1990.

Masters, John. *The Deceivers*. London: Michael Joseph, 1952.

Mayo, Katherine. *Mother India*. London: Jonathan Cape, 1927.

— (1929): *Slaves of the Gods*. New Delhi: Deep & Deep, 1988.

Moon, Sir Penderel. *The British Conquest and Dominion of India*, London: Duckworth, 1989.

Moorhouse, Geoffrey (1971). *Calcutta*. Harmondsworth: Penguin, 1974.

Nandy, Ashis (1994). "Sati as Profit Versus Sati as a Spectacle: The Public Debate on Roop Kanwar's Death." In: Hawley (Ed.), p. 131-49.

Narasimhan, Sakuntala (1990). *Sati: Widow Burning in India*. New York: Anchor Doubleday, 1992.

Oldenburg, Veena Talwar (1994). "The Roop Kanwar Case: Feminist Responses." In: Hawley (Ed.), p. 101-30.

— (1994a). "Comment: The Continuing Invention of the Sati Tradition." In: Hawley (Ed.), p. 159-73.

Pinney, Christopher. "Fuelling the Fire of the Sati Debate." In: *The Times Higher Education Supplement*, August 10, 2001, p. 30.

Pollitt, Katha. "Whose Culture?" In: *Is Multiculturalism Bad for Women?* Ed. Susan Moller Okin *et al.* Princeton, NJ: Princeton University Press, 1999, p. 27-30.

Polo, Marco (The Yule Edition). *The Book of Ser Marco Polo, the Venetian, Concerning the Kingdoms and the*

Marvels of the East. Trans. Henry Yule (1903). New York: Airmont, 1969.

Prentice, Eve-Ann. "Burnings That May Mask Murder." In: *The Times*, August 7, 2000, p. 6 f.

Rawlinson, H. G. (1925). *Intercourse between India and the Western World: From the Earliest Times to the Fall of Rome.* New Delhi: Uppal, 1992.

Rig-Veda (c.1300 B.C. or later).

(1) *Rig-Veda* (Sanskrit text with transcription). In: *Sacred-texts: The Internet Sacred Text Archive.* Web page, <http://www.sacred-texts.com/hin/rvsan/rvi10.htm>

(2) *Rig-Veda.* Trans. R. Griffith (1896). In: *Sacred-texts: The Internet Sacred Text Archive.* Web page, <http://www.sacred-texts.com/hin/rigveda/rv10018.htm> 10.08.2004)

Sen, Mala (2001). *Death by Fire: Sati, Dowry Death, and Female Infanticide in Modern India.* New Brunswick, NJ: Rutgers University Press, 2002.

Spivak, Gayatri Chakravorty. "Can the Subaltern Speak?" In: *Marxism and the Interpretation of Culture.* Ed. Cary Nelson & Lawrence Grossberg. Urbana, IL: University of Illinois Press, 1988, p. 271-311.

Thapar, Romila. *A History of India, Volume One.* Harmondsworth: Penguin, 1966.

Thompson, Edward. *Suttee: A Historical and Philosophical Enquiry into the Hindu Rite of Widow Burning.* Boston & New York: Houghton Mifflin, 1928.

Venkatesan, Radha. "Female Infanticide: Old Reasons, New Techniques." In: *The Hindu, online edition.* Web page, June 4, 2001, <http://www.hinduonnet.com/thehindu/2001/06/24/stories/04242233.htm> (30.08.2004)

Verne, Jules (1873). *Le Tour du monde en 80 jours* [*Around the World in Eighty Days*]. In: *Project Gutenberg.* Web page, <http://ibiblio.org/gutenberg/etext97/880jr07.txt>

Voltaire [François-Marie Arouet] (1747). *Zadig, ou la destinée: histoire orientale.* In: *Project Gutenberg.* Web page, <http://ibiblio.org/gutenberg/etext03/zadig10.txt>

Wadhwa, Soma. "Lambs to Slaughter." In: *Outlook.* Web page, October 18, 1995, <http://www.outlookindia.com/full.asp?fodname=19951018&fname=INVESTIGATION&sid=1o> (12.10.2002)

— (1996). "Glorifying a Gory Tradition." In: *Outlook*. Web page, December 11, 1996, <http://www.outlookindia.com/full.asp?fodname=19961211&fname=spotlight-&sid=1> (12.10.2002)

— (2002). "Waifs of the Gutter." In: *Outlook*. Web page, July 8, 2002, <http://www.outlookindia.com/full.asp?fodname=20020708&fname=Alwar+%28F%29&sid=1> (12.10.2002)

Wagner, Richard (1876). *Götterdämmerung*. In: *Gesammelte Schriften und Dichtungen*, Band 8 (1888). Hildesheim: Olms, 1976, pp.177-256.

Weinberger-Thomas, Catherine (1996). *Ashes of Immortality: Widow-Burning in India* [*Cendres d'immortalité*]. Trans. Jeffrey Mehlman & David Gordon White. Chicago & London: University of Chicago Press, 1999.

Wilkinson, Theon (1976). *Two Monsoons: The Life and Death of Europeans in India*. London: Duckworth, 1987.

FILMS

Around the World in 80 Days. Dir. Michael Anderson, 1956.

The Deceivers. Dir. Nicholas Meyer, 1988.

The Far Pavilions (TV). Dir. Peter Duffell, 1983.

VII.

THREE PANORAMIC NOVELS OF INDIA

Novels come in different shapes and sizes. For example, in a letter written in 1816, the year before her death, Jane Austen referred modestly to her own exquisite though narrowly-focused efforts as "the little bit (two inches wide) of ivory on which I work with so fine a brush" (Austen-Leigh, 1870, chapter 11). Then there are the huge panoramic canvases of novels like Tolstoy's *War and Peace*, which concern themselves with whole nations and epochs.

If there is a part of the world that is particularly suited to this latter type of novel, then surely it is India. The subcontinent, what was once British India and now comprises India, Pakistan, Bangladesh, and in some respects also Burma, Sri Lanka and the Maldives, is as large as Europe, with a similar, if not greater, number of geographical landscapes, cultures, ethnic groups, languages and religions, and with a comparably ancient, rich, and fascinating history. Even India proper is intimidating in its size and complexity.

The three novelists that I shall discuss have all attempted, in different ways, to reproduce something of the hugeness of India within a single book. They have all lived in the West, and have all chosen to write, at least in part, in English. This might seem paradoxical, but it is worth remembering that English is not a foreign language in India. There are many different languages spoken there, and the people who speak English fluently comprise only a few millions out of a billion or so – but they are people who *matter*: politicians, businessmen, scientists, artists, lawyers, and journalists, people who work internationally, in the media, in outsourcing, with foreigners within India, or with people from other regions of the country. The old colonial language English helps to bind the enormous country together, far more so than either the Hindu religion, which is regarded with suspicion by the large Islamic minority, or the most important truly indigenous language, Hindi, which has little appeal to speakers of Dravidian languages in the Indian south.

123

To write a "great novel of India" in an Indian language, whether Hindi, Punjabi, Tamil or any other, would be to risk its disappearance into local obscurity – however good the novel may actually be. There may indeed be more people in India who speak Marathi or Telugu than English-speakers in Britain or French-speakers in France, and more speakers of Malayalam than speakers of Italian, but who knows these languages and their literatures – even in translation – beyond the regions of India where they are at home? On the other hand, the potential readership for Indian books in English is internationally immense and even nationally, though not *numerically* greater (there are far more Hindi- than English-speakers in India), at least *wider* than for works in Indian languages.

There is another advantage to be gained from writing in English. Using a language that is not completely your own compels you to adopt a slightly different perspective and even distance to your material. It is a challenge to formulate and convey to an "alien" reader concepts and values that you may happen to hold but which were not developed within your culture or language. Indians who find it difficult to understand why the translations of excellent novels by regional Indian writers often win less praise internationally than Indian novels written in English sometimes forget how thematically narrow, how culturally blinkered, these local productions often seem to the non-local reader.

My chosen authors are coincidentally representatives of three major Indian religions – a Muslim, a Sikh, and a Hindu – although none of them are conventionally religious. I should like to approach the three panoramic novels in chronological order, which means starting with **Salman Rushdie** (b. 1947) and *Midnight's Children* (1981). This was an immense critical success, though the book has been perhaps more praised than read. It garnered the 1981 Booker, Britain's most prestigious literary prize, and in 1993 was chosen as "Booker of Bookers", the best of all Booker winners up to that date. Yet despite the quality of this and other Rushdie novels, there will probably be no Nobel Prize for Literature for him, because in many parts of the Islamic world this would be seen as a major affront to Islam. The reasons are well-known. Rushdie, the gadfly and provocateur, went a little too far with his portrayal of the Prophet Mohammed in the *The Satanic Verses* (1988), and in 1989 he was placed under sentence of death by Ayatollah Khomeini.

The eponymous Children are a symbol of India. Strange things happen to them, and they have magical powers. *Midnight's Children,* like Günter Grass's *Tin Drum* or the works of the Colombian novelist Gabriel García Márquez, is an outstanding example of the genre sometimes referred to as Magical Realism. The story has fantastic, even grotesque, elements, as in a dream, but the dream has an inner logic and an important message. Saleem Sinai, the central figure, stands for the new-born country: "thanks to the occult tyrannies of those blandly saluting clocks I had been mysteriously handcuffed to history, my destinies indissolubly chained to those of my country" (p. 9). He and the other children have come into the world at exactly twelve o'clock midnight on August 14, 1947, in the very second in which British India ceased to exist and the new independent India came into being.

In the final hours before independence, it is said that the future prime minister of India, Jawaharlal Nehru, was confused and disturbed by incoming reports of terrible atrocities against the Hindu and Sikh minorities in Lahore, in what was to be become (Islamic) Pakistan. He had very little time to prepare himself properly for the ceremony, and his renowned independence speech, much in the rhetorical style of Winston Churchill, is claimed to have been more or less an improvisation:

> Long years ago we made a tryst with destiny, and now the time comes when we shall redeem our pledge, not wholly or in full measure, but very substantially. At the stroke of the midnight hour, while the world sleeps, India will awake to life and freedom. A moment comes, which comes but rarely in history, when we step out from the old to the new, when an age ends, and when the soul of a nation, long suppressed, finds utterance.[...]

At the dawn of history, India started on her un-
ending quest, and trackless centuries are filled with her
striving and the grandeur of her successes and her fail-
ures. Through good- and ill-fortune alike she has never
lost sight of that quest or forgotten the ideal which
gave her strength. We end today a period of ill-fortune
and India discovers herself again. [...]
This is no time for petty and destructive criticism, no time for ill-will or blaming others. We have to
build the noble mansion of free India where all her
children may dwell (in MacArthur, 1992, p. 238 f.).

The speech is magnificent, but it gives an account of
the Indian past that is untrue, and a programme for the future
that the new country will scarcely be able to fulfil. *Midnight's
Children* is a commentary on and a deconstruction of this
famous speech. The birth of India entailed the creation of a
mammoth, heterogeneous but Hindu-dominated country such
as had not existed either before the Muslim incursions or afterwards, during the rule of such Islamic dynasties as the Sultans of Delhi and the Mughal emperors. Before the British
consolidated their colonial possessions in the subcontinent,
there had been no such country as "India". Three of India's
great cities – Calcutta (now Kolkata), Bombay (now Mum-
bai) and Madras (now Chennai) – were colonial foundations;
only Delhi was truly Indian. When the Indian independence
movement, the Indian National Congress, was founded in
1885, prominent among its members were Britons like Allan
Octavian Hume.
Like India itself, Saleem has a British father. But for
a hundred pages readers are hoodwinked into believing that
they know who Saleem's parents and grandparents are – and
then comes the big confusion. There are so many of them,
and they were all involved in helping Saleem to be born.
Perhaps his natural father is an Englishman! Like all the
other Children, he is a child of the Indian past, unable to
deny any of his fathers, not even the British one:

In fact, all over the new India, the dream we all
shared, children were being born who were only par-

tially the offspring of their parents – the children of midnight were also the children of the time: fathered, you understand, by history. It can happen. Especially in a country which is itself a sort of dream (p. 118).

There is no such thing, no such country, as India, except an India that is dreamt:

> Rumours in the city; "the statue galloped last night". ... "And the stars are unfavourable!" ...But despite these signs of ill-omen, the city was poised, with a new myth glinting in the corners of its eyes. August in Bombay: a month of festivals, the month of Krishna's birthday and Coconut Day; and this year – fourteen hours to go, thirteen, twelve – there was an extra festival on the calendar, a new myth to celebrate, because a nation which had never previously existed was about to win its freedom, catapulting us into a world which, although it had five thousand years of history, although it had invented the game of chess and traded with Middle Kingdom Egypt, was nevertheless quite imaginary; into a mythical land, a country which would never exist except by the efforts of phenomenal collective will – except in a dream we all agreed to dream; it was a mass fantasy shared in varying degrees by Bengali and Punjabi, Madrasi and Jat, and would periodically need the sanctification and renewal which can only be provided by rituals of blood. India, the new myth – a collective fiction in which anything was possible, a fable rivalled only by the two other mighty fantasies: money and God.
> I have been, in my time the living proof of the fabulous nature of this collective dream [...] (p. 112).

Both of them, Saleem and his country, will have a difficult ride. The hour of birth is also the beginning of an abortion – the abortion of the idea of a tolerant, pluralistic nation on Indian soil. In the end, it is the terrifying widow Indira Gandhi who rules the country by Emergency legisla-

127

tion, and the Children are forcibly sterilised; *hope* is cut out of them too.

> [...] what I learned from the Widow's Hand is that those who would be gods fear no one so much as other potential deities; and that, that and that only, is why we, the magical children of midnight, were hated feared destroyed by the Widow, who was not only Prime Minister of India but also aspired to be Devi, the Mother-goddess in her most terrible aspect, possessor of the shakti of the gods, a multi-limbed divinity with a centre-parting and schizophrenic hair... (p. 438).

Midnight's Children is a demanding novel, an Indian roller-coaster of the senses. Like Indian food, it is rich, mysterious, aromatic, and (for some people) hard to digest. It is full of wordplays, parodies and linguistic experiments, changing landscapes and hectic events. The identification of Saleem with India works in both directions. He embodies the world of India, but in order to understand him, or anyone, you have to be aware of his world in all its complexity. "To understand just one life, you have to swallow the world" (p.109). In his essay "Imaginary Homelands" (1982), Rushdie admits that with *Midnight's Children*, a book that was written in North London exile, he was trying to regain his own past:

> It is probably not too romantic to say that [my revisit to Bombay] was when my novel *Midnight's Children* was really born; when I realised how much I wanted to restore the past to myself, not in the faded greys of old family-album snapshots, but whole, in CinemaScope and glorious Technicolor (p. 9 f.).

Like Saleem, he too was born in 1947, although eight weeks earlier than the magical Children.

The second of our panoramic works, the highly readable *Delhi* (1990), is a quite different sort of book. **Khushwant Singh** (b. 1915) is a member of the Sikh religious minority. The Sikhs are stereotyped in India as being robust, athletic, warlike, fiery and (it must be said) somewhat sim-ple-minded. Hot-headed, their brains boiling under their tur-bans, they drive taxis, fight India's wars, and represent their country as sportsmen. Every male Sikh carries the name "Singh", or "lion", and as a grave insult they may refer to someone who is perhaps more quiet and bookish than them-selves as a *papad pulwaun* ("he who does battle with cook-ies"). Khushwant Singh is therefore a paradox – a Sikh intel-lectual and writer (who has also been a High Court lawyer, diplomat, historian, academic – at Oxford and Princeton, among other universities – and a member of parliament). Among his published works are histories, novels, short sto-ries, religious commentary and anthologies. He is not one of the Sikhs who drive taxis like a maniac, but he has many of the traditional Sikh qualities: he is direct, open, friendly and of a lively temperament; he loves women and whiskey – a collection of his work appeared under the title *Sex, Scotch and Scholarship: Selected Writings* (1992); and he has a tongue like a whiplash – a recently published collection of his newspaper columns was entitled *Khushwant Singh's Big Book of Malice* (2000).

Delhi was a sensational bestseller, sold out through advance orders before it actually appeared. Khushwant Singh had taken twenty-five years to write the novel, and put into it "all I had in me as a writer: love, lust, sex, hate, vendetta and violence – and above all, tears" (p. v). His narrator is also a writer and journalist, and an unpaid tourist guide on the side (especially when it is a matter of revealing to impressionable females the best that his beloved Delhi has to offer...). The history of Delhi is told chronologically in dramatic, often erotic, first-person accounts. In "A Note from the Author", he reveals: "History provided me with the skeleton. I covered it with flesh and injected blood and a lot of seminal fluid into it" (p. vi; curiously, the "seminal fluid" has disappeared from at least one European translation of *Delhi*). The historical episodes are interspersed between accounts of events in the present and inspired by everyday things that happen to the narrator. For example, the narrator's "girlfriend" nags him because he has achieved so little financially since coming to the city. She compares him with successful Punjabi entrepreneurs, and there then follows a story about the hardworking small businessmen who came to Delhi at the beginning of the twentieth century, to help to build the new capital city New Delhi, and who enriched themselves pleasantly in the process.

The "girlfriend" Bhagmati is not a woman but a *hijda*, a transsexual. There are many thousands of such people in India, many of them working in entertainment, for example as prostitutes, singers or dancers. They are an intrinsic element in urban everyday life in India. The curse of a *hijda* is particularly feared, and so one never sends one away empty-handed. The narrator in *Delhi* has two great passions, for the whore Bhagmati and for the city of Delhi. "They have two things in common: they are lots of fun. And they are sterile" (p. 30). The historical episodes end in frustration, defeat, resignation, exile, or death. On the other hand, the novel itself is bursting with life: people fight, make love, write poetry, and there is a whole chapter about farting. The descriptions are both sensitive and sensuous. Here, for instance, is a gorgeous evocation of daybreak in Delhi, including a characteristic power failure:

> Power Cut. No light, no fan. I come out into my patch of garden and flop into a canechair. It's hot, humid, dark and still. There are a few stars, but they are very very far away. And there are too many mosquitoes. I think angry thoughts. I will write letters to the papers about delays at the airport, the manners of customs inspectors, cheating by cab-drivers, the inefficiency of the electricity company, Delhi telephones, Delhi water supply....Then I think of Bhagmati. I wonder how much whoring she has done while I have been away. She likes to tell me of her exploits because she knows it rouses my desire for her. I sit in the dark many hours. I am angry, I am wanton. Then less angry, more wanton. A pale, old moon wanders into the sky. A light goes up in the temple behind my apartment. The electricity is back when it is not needed. I get up and drag my feet into the sitting room.

I switch on the table-lamp. 5.15 a.m. I throw open the window. The curtains flutter. A cool breeze fragrant with the *madhumalati* which covers the outside wall drives away the dank fuzz of yesterday's dead air. I sink into my armchair and gaze out of the window. Streetlights go off with a silent bang. Through the foliage of the mulberry tree appears the grey dawn.

Flying foxes wing their soundless way back to perch on massive *arjun* trees. The old lady who lives in the apartment above mine slish-sloshes along the road. She stops by my hibiscus hedge, looks around to see if anyone is looking, quickly plucks some flowers, thrusts them in her *dupatta* and slish-sloshes on towards the temple. Her old man follows her. He also stops by my hedge, looks around to see if anyone is listening, presses his paunch, and lets out a long, painful fart. He walks on with a lighter step and a "who did that?" look on his face. A light goes on in the opposite block. A woman draws the curtains, ties her untidy hair into a bun and stretches her arms towards me. More lights are switched on and off. The morning star is barely visible in the pink sky. Crows begin cawing to each other. Sparrows start quarrelling in the mulberry tree. The muezzin's voice rises to the heavens. Temple bells peal to awaken the gods from their slumbers. The milkman cycles round the block with a noisy clanging of milk-cans. Another cyclist follows tinkling his bell and shouting "*Paperwalla! Ishtaitman, Taim of India, Hindustan Taim, Express, Herald, paperwalla!*" I hear the shush of papers being pushed under my door. I stay in my armchair. The morning breeze wafts the light of dawn into the room. It is cool, fragrant, pregnant with sadness and longing; it is the *bad-i-saba* – the morning breeze – sacred to lovers. And I am back in my beloved city (p. 6-8).

The closing pages of the novel are less appealing, re-telling as they do the grim events of November 1984 after the murder of Indira Gandhi by her Sikh bodyguards. Rabid supporters of the dead leader stormed through Sikh residential areas, murdering some 5,000 Sikhs as they went. The authorities seemed helpless to prevent the violence. Rajiv Gandhi is claimed to have said, chillingly, "When a big tree falls, the earth around it shakes." I spoke to a Sikh survivor of the massacre, who had witnessed the bestial killing of almost everyone in his street before the chance arrival of a local train packed with unfortunate Sikhs distracted the mob for long enough for him to be able to escape. Khushwant Singh too escaped the killings. His narrator watches from hiding as his neighbours are tortured and set alight. The proud Sikh, who has wetted himself in fear, is saved by the *hijda*. He notices how Bhagmati has grown old and fat, with "sparse hair daubed with henna. No teeth. Squashed mouth. Hair-bristle about her chin. Is this the same Bhagmati I had lusted after most of my lustful years?" (p. 386).

Delhi is a panoramic novel in the sense that, though focusing on just one city, it makes it a microcosm of India, and opens up a vista of 700 years of history. And it is more than just a collection of historical anecdotes. It moves with cumulative power towards a kind of emotional stock-taking, a declaration of love for a city, albeit the declaration of an old man. It is life-enhancing, yet with the bittersweet awareness that most human efforts lead to nothing, or at least not to what you had hoped for. But you have the memories, and the history of a great city can be reconstructed from them.

The third of our panoramic novels offers a rather different approach to the hugeness of India, this time synchronic rather than diachronic. At a given moment, the fate of the nation is shown – on an epic scale, cities and country, families, castes, rulers and professions are lit up in a wide-angle snapshot that catches the whole country and its fate through the interwoven destinies of a large number of vivid characters.

Vikram Seth (b. 1952) is a Hindu, an economist and a poet. As a child, he was considered a genius. He learnt Chinese well-enough within a year to be able to write poetry in it. He lived in California, and published a highly-praised satirical novel in verse, *The Golden Gate* (1986), about the Californian lifestyle. He became internationally known for his novel *A Suitable Boy* (1993), which is reputedly longer than the Bible (though still 700 pages shorter than its first draft). It has been compared with the works of Tolstoy und Dostoyevsky; it is supposedly the longest individual novel of the twentieth century, and if not the longest novel ever written in English, certainly the longest since Samuel Richardson's *Clarissa*, more than 250 years ago. The author himself has made fun of the fuss over the size of the book – "A very large novel written by a very small Indian" (Gavron, 1999) – and in a verse-form "Word of Thanks" prefacing the novel, he concludes: "Buy me, before good sense insists / You'll strain your purse and sprain your wrists" (p. ix). His novel was two feet high in typescript, and the paperback edition weighed almost a kilogram.

Seth documents important and characteristic events of the period after Indian independence, the "Nehru years", with remarkable accuracy and empathy. Although he describes cruel political and religious conflicts, the tone of the novel is essentially warm-hearted and kindly, with domestic misunderstandings and confusion in love being the central themes of the story. It is *War and Peace* as a gentler Jane Austen might have written it.

The main setting is the fictional provincial city of Brahmpur ("the city of God"), which offers a microcosm of India. The plot is concerned with the doings and interaction of four extended families, with their various friends and acquaintances. Young Lata Mehra is in want of a husband. She has her own opinions on the matter, and is unwilling simply to accept an arranged marriage; on the other hand, she has no wish to upset her widowed mother, Rupa Mehra, whose views on what might constitute a "suitable boy" are not identical with her daughter's. Apart from a number of comic grotesques, there are three serious candidates for Lata's affections: Kabir, the Muslim fellow student whom she loves, but whose faith makes him wholly unacceptable unless Lata is prepared to break with her family; Amit, her cousin from Calcutta, who is amusing but wholly out of touch with reality – this is probably a self-portrait of the author; and Haresh, a strong-willed and ambitious young businessman who is unfortunately lacking in all those qualities – wit, charm, and imagination – that Lata most values.

A novel of this length must maintain a certain plot tension. It would be unfair to reveal what choice Lata finally makes. She has almost 1,500 pages in which to decide, and along the way there are unexpected twists and interventions, and massive conflicts. In the following scene, for example, Rupa Mehra has heard that her daughter has been spotted going for a walk with an unknown young man. She is determined to find out more:

"What's his name?"

"Kabir," said Lata, growing pale.

"Kabir what?"

Lata stood still and didn't answer. A tear rolled down her cheek.

Mrs. Rupa Mehra was in no mood for sympathy. What were all these ridiculous tears? She caught hold of Lata's ear and twisted it. Lata gasped.

"He has a name, doesn't he? What is he – Kabir Lal, Kabir Mehra – or what? Are you waiting for the tea to get cold? Or have you forgotten?"

Lata closed her eyes.

"Kabir Durrani," she said, and waited for the house to come tumbling down.

The three deadly syllables had their effect. Mrs. Rupa Mehra clutched at her heart, opened her mouth in silent horror, looked unseeingly around the room, and sat down.

Savita [*Lata's sister*] rushed to her immediately. Her own heart was beating far too fast.

One last faint possibility struck Mrs. Rupa Mehra. "Is he a Parsi?" she asked weakly, almost pleadingly. The thought was odious but not so calamitously horrifying. But a look at Savita's face told her the truth.

"A Muslim!" said Mrs. Rupa Mehra more to herself now than to anyone else. "What did I do in my past life that I have brought this upon my beloved daughter?"

Savita was standing near her and held her hand. Mrs. Rupa Mehra's hand was inert as she stared in front of her. Suddenly she became aware of the gentle

134

curve of Savita's stomach and fresh horrors came to her mind.

She stood up again. "Never, never, never – " she said.

By now Lata, having conjured up the image of Kabir in her mind, had gained a little strength. She opened her eyes. Her tears had stopped and there was a defiant set to her mouth.

"Never, never, absolutely not – dirty, violent, cruel, lecherous –"

"Like Talat Khala?" demanded Lata. "Like Uncle Shafi? Like the Nawab Sahib of Baitar? Like Firoz and Imtiaz?"

"Do you want to marry him?" cried Mrs. Rupa Mehra in a fury.

"Yes!" said Lata, carried away, and angrier by the second.

"He'll marry you – and next year he'll say "Talaq talaq talaq" [*"divorce, divorce, divorce"*] and you'll be out on the streets. You obstinate, stupid girl! You should drown yourself in a handful of water for sheer shame."

"I *will* marry him," said Lata, unilaterally (p.196 f.).

Kabir is good-looking, intelligent, athletic, and of noble character. He has kissed Lata and won her love. But as a Muslim he is out of the question as a suitable candidate for Lata's hand, at least as far as her mother is concerned.

However, his two main rivals also have major disqualifying characteristics. Amit comes from an impossible, chaotic Bengali family. Chatty, witty, and overemotional, the Calcuttans in the novel are a complete contrast to the stolid citizens of Brahmpur. Amit's selfish sister Meenakshi has married Lata's arrogant, snobbishly anglophile brother Arun – and cheats on her husband outrageously. Amit himself is a successful minor poet, a perfectly acceptable career to follow in a city as obsessed with culture and the arts as Calcutta, the "Paris of India"; however, Lata's mother is, perhaps predictably, less than impressed:

She looked at Amit, and thought: "Poet, wastrel!" He has never earned an honest rupee in his life. I will not have all my grandchildren speaking Bengali! Suddenly she remembered that the last time Amit had dropped Lata home, she had had flowers in her hair (p. 527).

Haresh, on the other hand, is a man who wears silk shirts, fawn-coloured gaberdine trousers, and flashy two-tone shoes, which he obviously regards as being rather smart. His mouth is red from chewing *paan*, or betelnut, the Indian equivalent of chewing-gum. "Paan did not go at all well with fawn gaberdine and a silk shirt. In fact paan did not go at all well with her idea of a husband" (p. 617). Haresh belongs to the same caste group as the Mehras, but he works in the shoe industry – with *leather* – which calls his caste purity very much into question.

Another important young man in the story is Maan, who as a notorious playboy and ne'er-do-well is established as "unsuitable" right from the start. Ironically, while the "suitable" young men are being allowed to make fools of themselves, Maan is slipped for a while into the role of the romantic lead. Himself a Hindu, he falls in love with the famous Muslim singer and courtesan Saeeda Bai, but also becomes emotionally and probably sexually involved with a young Muslim nobleman, Firoz. This rather surprising bisexuality is not only presented in a plausible way, but is also an integral plot factor, almost leading to tragedy and the ruin of two of the families.

Maan the irresponsible hedonist risks his own life to save his friend Firoz from a bloodthirsty Hindu mob, putting himself between the frightened Muslim and a drunken thug who is wielding a bloodstained, metal-tipped stick. The relationship between the two young men is an important symbol of friendship and tolerance across the barrier of religion, a message that the young republics of India and Pakistan still have to learn.

Vikram Seth's sources are eclectic and international, and perhaps this is one reason why *A Suitable Boy* initially failed to make a great impression on some Indian critics. For a late twentieth-century novel it was also deeply anachronistic. Jane Austen has already been mentioned as a possible inspiration. The influence of the great nineteenth-century Realists is obvious; indeed, nothing could be further from Magical Realism than Seth's sober, well-crafted prose. Echoes of another British author, Rudyard Kipling, are evident (for example) in the treatment of the courtesan, Saeeda Bai. Other elements, such as the small town bickerings and confusions in Brahmpur, are reminiscent of the great Indian writer R. K. Narayan. Seth, who has published works in British, American *and* Indian English, is hard to pigeonhole as an Indian writer, but *A Suitable Boy* is undoubtedly an Indian novel. This becomes apparent in the ending of the book. Without revealing too much, it will suffice to say that the decision that Lata reaches is one that many, perhaps even most, Western readers will find surprising or actually shocking, but in the Indian context her decision is completely understandable. Through the choice that Lata makes, she reaffirms her Indian cultural identity. At this point, the Western reader is likely to experience an abrupt culture shock and be faced with the need to think once again about Indian behaviour patterns and values, a process for which this huge novel provides abundant material. It is this suddenly confrontational aspect of *A Suitable Boy* which rescues its main storyline from being ultimately no more than a charming but long-drawn-out romantic comedy with a conventional happy ending.

It would be going too far to suggest that Lata is an intentional symbol of India "at the crossroads", or that her decision is a metaphor for the choice of direction that India should supposedly take. Vikram Seth is much too concerned with his characters as individuals. Lata is a human being in a particular social and historical context, that of India in the Fifties, who is pursuing her personal happiness. Half a century later, she would have other opportunities – she might be riding a Vespa, working in a call centre or an advertising agency, doing something exciting in the world of international finance, or perhaps an M.B.A. – and she would possibly make a different choice of husband. But it would be *her* choice, made for *her* reasons, which we might still need to be helped to understand.

REFERENCES

Austen-Leigh, James Edward (1870). *A Memoir of Jane Austen by Her Nephew.* Web page, <http://labrocca. com/ja/mja-ch11.html> (Accessed 30.08.2004)

Gavron, Jeremy. "A Suitable Joy." In: *Guardian Unlimited,* March 27, 1999. Web page, <http://www.guardian. co.uk/Archive/Article/0,4273,3845046,00.html>(30.08.2004)

MacArthur, Brian (Ed.) (1992). *The Penguin Book of Twentieth-Century Speeches.* Harmondsworth: Penguin, 1999.

Richardson, Samuel (1747-48). *Clarissa; or, The History of a Young Lady.* 4 vols. London/New York: Dent/Dutton, 1932.

Rushdie, Salman (1981). *Midnight's Children.* London: Pan, 1982.

— (1982). "Imaginary Homelands." In: *Imaginary Homelands: Essays and Criticism, 1981-1991* (1991). London/Harmondsworth: Granta/Penguin, 1992, p. 9-21.

— (1988). *The Satanic Verses.* New York: Viking Penguin, 1989.

Seth, Vikram (1986). *The Golden Gate.* London: Faber & Faber, 1999.

— (1993). *A Suitable Boy.* London: Phoenix, 1994.

Singh, Khushwant. *Delhi.* New Delhi: Penguin, 1990.

— (1992). *Sex, Scotch and Scholarship: Selected Writings.* New Delhi: HarperCollins, 2004.

—. *Khushwant Singh's Big Book of Malice.* New Delhi: Penguin, 2000.

VIII.

GOING PLACES, MEETING PEOPLE

There are two basic responses to strangers: *xenophobia* and *xenophilia*. Most western cultures are distinctly xenophobic, which means that they tend to view foreigners and strangers with caution, mistrust, dislike or aggression. The old Irish saying, that "A stranger is a friend whom you haven't met yet", is applied less often than the Japanese saying, "When you see a stranger, it is safer to assume that he is a thief." Education, or experience with strangers at home or abroad, *can* but will not *necessarily* correct this negative viewpoint. For example, when students are sent for a period of study abroad, they often report back on their experiences among the foreigners with enthusiasm, sometimes even delight. On the other hand there are those who insist that what they experienced only served to confirm the prejudices that they already had about that particular culture and its people. American students resident at a major German university coined the term "The German Death Look" (or "Medusa Look" or "Death Ray") for the grim stares that they felt they were getting from the local townspeople (Obermann, 2003, p. 45 f.). It makes no odds that there is a quite banal explanation for the behaviour that the Americans had become aware of – Central Europeans, unlike Americans or Southeast Asians, are "occasional" rather than "contact smilers" (Jürgen Beneke), that is, a smile has to be motivated by something, and is not part of normal contact behaviour. But the effect remains the same, whatever the cause of the behaviour may be, and it is so easy for the behaviour of strangers to be misunderstood. There is a joke going the rounds among sociologists: one student tells another, "I hate foreigners, because they've turned me into someone who hates foreigners!" (Outhwaite, *Toward*).

Anyone who is taking the trouble to read this essay is very likely to belong to those who would agree that the model for interaction with strangers should include tolerance, a lack of prejudice, and a hefty dose of goodwill. Meeting those standards, however, is a tall order. Of course we are embarrassed when a stuttering, helpless foreigner is bullied by petty officials, and yet here at home, in our own backyard, we want things to be done *our* way and according to *our* habits and values.

Between the two extreme positions of, on the one hand, politically correct, uncritical acceptance of all cultural manifestations of any kind – the lawyer defending his client, a father who had murdered his rebellious daughter and dismembered her body, with the argument that "they do that sort of thing where he comes from, it's part of his culture" (although the man had lived in Western Europe for thirty years) – and, on the other hand, hate-filled, chauvinistic rejection of *anything* unfamiliar, there is a spectrum of different types of response to alterity. The possibilities become especially apparent when people *travel*, and travel writing and literature provide a rich mine of material to illustrate them.

In earlier times, such contacts were rare. People needed a good reason to travel, and didn't expect to encounter strangers on a regular basis. The reasons for travelling – trading, going on a holiday or a pilgrimage, seeking information, waging war – are still valid today, although the numbers have increased a million-fold, but there are also new ways of making contact with strangers, in the virtual marketplace of the media and the net of the global village.

Not many people went on journeys. There were "resident strangers", *i.e.*, ethnic minority groups, but those which had *not* been enslaved or massacred tended to lead a fragile, vulnerable existence within the broader host community, a situation which is still the norm in many parts of the world today. Exotic visitors were a sensational event, a fact which helps to explain the resonance in Western art over many hundreds of years of the Biblical story of the Three Kings.

Being puzzled or fascinated by visiting strangers is an age-old phenomenon, but contact with strangers on their own territory is even more deeply disturbing. The idea of interacting with foreigners on the basis of equality was probably beyond the comprehension of most people. The normal attitude was one of ethnocentrism of the most primitive kind. This exaggerated self-pride can be found in many cultures,

140

and even today it is not far below the surface when the French refer to the benefits of *civilisation française*, the Russians to the uniqueness of the "Russian soul", the Chinese to China's central position in the world as the "Middle Kingdom", the Japanese to their unique descent from the gods, and so on. It was given robust expression by the British imperialist Cecil Rhodes in his *Confession of Faith* (1877) when he wrote: "I contend that we are the finest race in the world and that the more of the world we inhabit the better it is for the human race." And even in the twilight years of the British Empire there were prominent Britons who were less than happy with the idea of having to make compromises in dealing with foreigners. When in 1951 Selwyn Lloyd was appointed as Foreign Secretary (equivalent to the Secretary of State in America), the following conversation is said to have occurred between Lloyd and his Prime Minister, Winston Churchill. Lloyd attempted to explain why he was unqualified for the ministerial position:

"But sir, I think there must be some mistake, I've never been to a foreign country, I don't speak any foreign languages, I don't like foreigners." "Young man," [Churchill replied], "these all seem to me to be positive advantages" (Thorpe, 1989, p. 153).

Rather than trying to cope with foreigners in an intelligent and tolerant manner, many people preferred simply to *despise and abuse* them. There were three main reasons for this: it was partly in order to create a common identity and feelings of solidarity within one's own culture (the "in-group") by demonstratively setting up unattractive alternatives (or "out-groups"); it was, in situations of conquest and colonisation, in order to make it easier to dominate, enslave and exploit other peoples by first dehumanising them; and it was also, on a more trivial level, in order to use them as material for humour ("Irish jokes") and literary wit. (And, far from excluding each other, these three mechanisms overlap quite considerably.)

Foreign travel was an excellent way to rediscover and *assert the advantages of one's own culture*. Around 1780,

John Richard, who made it as far as St. Petersburg in Russia, declared that "from every nation, from even every circumstance, travellers will find many occasions to admire the constitution and comforts of their own country" (quoted in Black, 1992, p. 232). A contemporary of his, John Villiers, was of the opinion (1788) that

> every young man ought to go abroad, to make him the more attached to his own country. I find everything here [*in France*] so extremely inferior, that I glow with pride and rapture, when I think I am an Englishman (p. 294).

Richard Rigby (1776) returned from France with the emphatic opinion that that country was "a dunghill, not fit for a gentleman to live in" (p. 159). No doubt there were often personal reasons for being dissatisfied and not liking either the place or its inhabitants. In the sixteenth century, Ralph Sadler, the English ambassador to Scotland, wrote to London: "Under the sun lives not more beastly and unreasonable people than here be of all degrees" (Johnson, 1972, p. 148). The comparative approach often flourishes in times when national self-confidence is at a low, for instance in Germany after the humiliation of defeat in the First World War, as members of the "Cultural Studies" movement went in search of that elusive thing "Germanness" (*Deutschtum*), a positive and characteristic national identity, by drawing comparisons between the Germans and other races.

Nor should we forget the religious factor: heathens, infidels and unbelievers are assumed by their very nature to be inferior. For example, the anonymous lady missionary author of *Near Home; or, Europe Described* (1849, revised edition 1894), F. L. Bevan, described Turkey as the European country that she would *least* like to live in, because it had such a bad religion (p. 32); she felt sorry for the Greeks, who lived in a charming country but had the misfortune to have the Turks as their neighbours (p. 35); and so on in much the same vein.

I have already suggested that there is a connection between the scorn felt for strange people and customs and the production of humour. Humour is the key to travel literature: "Oh God, aren't they weird!" the author writes, and takes it from there. What Lenček and Bosker (1998) describe as being characteristic of travel accounts of the early Victorian period, that the travellers venture among people whose views on such matters as hygiene, correct social behaviour towards members of the opposite sex, table manners or simply the appropriate way of talking in public differ drastically from one's own (p. 120), provides the material for a huge number of literary or journalistic travel reports. This is just as true of, for example, Tobias Smollett in the eighteenth century as it is of modern authors like Paul Theroux, whose *Great Railway Bazaar* (1975) is an almost continuous mockery of the people whose countries he travels through, or P. J. O'Rourke, whose notorious report from South Korea, *Seoul Brothers* (1988), begins with the following flourish (in his function as a "foreign correspondent" for his magazine, the author is reporting on a political demonstration):

> When the kid in the front row at the rally bit off the tip of his little finger and wrote, KIM DAE JUNG, in blood on his fancy white ski jacket – I think that was the first time I ever really felt like a foreign correspondent. I mean, here was something really fucking foreign (p. 93).

Noticeably, it is not the peculiar Korean who is the central focus of this scene, but the effect that his peculiar behaviour has on the author. O'Rourke is following here in the footsteps of the French exoticist writer Pierre Loti, whose novels, once world bestsellers, tend now to be the object of derision, and who wrote in the dedication at the beginning of his most famous work, *Madame Chrysanthème* (1887), that the book was not about the Japanese girl Chrysanthème, but about "*myself, Japan,* and the *effect* produced on me by that country" ("*Moi,* le *Japon,* et l'*effet* que ce pays m'a produit") (p. 5, see also Jarman, 1998, p.161). Not all too much has changed in travel writing since the days of Loti – instead of being concerned with the alien Other, a distorting mirror in which with an honest gaze to discover truths about the Self, the writer circles tremulously in increasingly solipsistic self-preoccupation.

If (for hundreds of years) travel was such a strenuous and nerve-wracking business, and the strangers that one met so unappealing, why did people do it? The easiest answer is that most people *didn't* travel, unless it was absolutely necessary, and that in any case those who did were usually men – except for trips to market, most women only left home as a bride, a hostage or a slave. But there was one social institution that could make travelling substantially more comfortable, and since it is has almost died out in the Western world we should perhaps spare a few moments to consider it.

In traditional societies, in which the infrastructure is weak and travel a rare and even dangerous undertaking, the interaction between strangers such as may occur on a journey is often governed by a valuable social mechanism of temporary and reciprocal social obligation known as *hospitality*. The world of the Homeric Greeks was just such a society. *Xenia*, the treatment of guests, was a special concern of Zeus, the mightiest of the gods. In Book 14 of Homer's *Odyssey*, Eumaios, Odysseus's swineherd, at first fails to recognise his master, who is disguised as a beggar, but still welcomes him, as the rules of *xenia* require: "Stranger, it is not right for me to slight a stranger, even though one of less account than you were to come: for all strangers and beggars are from Zeus" [...] (p. 41). Centuries later, in 466 B.C., the cunning Athenian statesman Themistocles could still exploit what was by then an archaic tradition of guest-friendship to escape from mortal danger. On the run, Themistocles was forced to seek refuge under the roof of his bitter enemy Admetus, King of the Molossians. The historian Plutarch describes what happened:

> [Themistocles] threw himself upon the [king's] mercy, by making himself a suppliant to Admetus in a peculiar fashion which is found in no other country. He took the king's young son in his arms and prostrated himself before the hearth, this being the form of supplication which the Molossians consider the most sol-

emn and which it is virtually impossible to refuse (p. 100).

In the more ordered world of the *Pax Romana* there was less need for the traditional rules of hospitality. Many of those who travelled would be on state business, and they were given priority in the network of inns and guesthouses that stretched across the road system of the empire; or they might be traders, who could stay with business contacts or friends of friends; or, if they were wealthy Romans, they might have villas or town houses of their own in some of the more attractive destinations. There were inns for travellers in almost every city, often with an unenviable reputation, but Roman law gave the traveller some limited protection by holding the innkeeper accountable (up to a point) for thefts that took place under his roof (Casson, 1974, p. 204 f.). Nor was *xenia* completely extinct, as the following story, about the rich and famous philosopher Antonius Polemon (*ca.* 88-144), shows.

Polemon's pride, and the increased self-confidence derived from knowing that he had the favour of [the emperor] Hadrian, gave him courage to respond to the provincial governor and later emperor [Antoninus], who had quartered himself in Polemon's house without his knowledge, by showing his unwelcome guest the door. Antoninus had perhaps meant well, in choosing what was both the best house in Smyrna and the home of its foremost resident, in that he considered that Polemon might otherwise have been offended, if the governor had selected someone else for the honour of his visit. But, asserting the right of freedom from billeting that had been granted to him, [Polemon] demanded – in the middle of the night – that he move to another house (*RE*, p. 1335 f.).

Things could have turned out really badly for Polemon. Soon afterwards, Antoninus became emperor and the philosopher was required to present himself at court in Rome. But Antoninus embraced him and, no doubt with a

145

twinkle in his eye, announced loudly: "Provide [Polemon] with somewhere to stay, and let no-one dare to evict him from his lodgings!" (p. 1336).

This little story tells us something about the calm, good-natured character of Antoninus, especially when he is contrasted with the intemperate Polemon, but it also draws much of its point from the comparison between Polemon's arrogant disregard for the laws of hospitality and Antoninus's generosity towards his guest.

In the ancient world it was generally the wealthy who (voluntarily) went on journeys. Just as you can today, you could improve your social status by taking in famous sights like the "Seven Wonders of the World". It was not so very different when, in the eighteenth century, the British, by that time one of the world's richest nations, popularised the so-called "Grand Tour". And foreign travel was still a strenuous, sometimes dangerous, matter, not to be undertaken lightly. Which leads us to an interesting question – in making the decision to travel abroad, which factors did the potential traveller see as more important: "pull factors" like the attractiveness of the destination or "push factors" like the social pressure, engendered by snobbery, to go on such a journey? On April 11th, 1776, the great Dr. Samuel Johnson announced to his friends over lunch: "A man who has not been in Italy, is always conscious of an inferiority, from his not having seen what it is expected a man should see. The grand object of travelling is to see the shores of the Mediterranean" (Boswell, vol. 3). But many continental Europeans found the motivation of the British travellers hard to understand, as William Bennett discovered (October, 1785):

Nothing surprises foreigners so much as the numbers of our countrymen that travel. The Swiss in particular often asked me how it happened, and said our country must be very unhealthy that everyone was so eager to get out of it (quoted in Black, p. 9 f.).

(In 1840, Théophile Gautier made the observation that the English were everywhere – except in London (Withey, 1997, p. 62). And today, given the massive preponderance of non-British faces on Oxford Street, one might think that not much has changed in the last 165 years!)

Although it was normal to complain about the faults and peculiarities of the foreigners, the comparison between familiar and foreign was not always favourable towards the former. There were travellers and travel writers who used foreign cultures as a *touchstone* for criticising their own. Just as Tacitus had done with the ancient Germans, they attributed to the foreigners all kinds of virtues that they believed had, unfortunately, become rare among their own people. However, these admirable figures – wise mandarins or holy men, noble savages, generous pirates or bandits, dignified sultans – tended to be literary abstractions rather than flesh-and-blood people.

In similar fashion, others *exoticised the Other*, in other words, they fantasised the Other as embodying or acting out certain fascinating or forbidden things, often of a sexual nature. Whole subgenres of popular literature, art or the cinema have been powered by these projections of unfulfilled Western yearning onto "exotic" cultures, including (to name just a few) the South Seas myth of free love under the palm-trees, the harem obsession of French "Orientalist" artists in the nineteenth century, or the sinister Dr. Fu-Manchu (see Jarman, 1998, p. 81 f.).

A more constructive attitude to take is the view that your own culture is hard to understand until you have had some experience outside it – *self-definition in the mirror of the Other*. The interaction with alien peoples and cultures is a process that can lead you to your own cultural identity. Around 1787, Arthur Young declared that his foreign travels had taught him that, "to know our own country well, we must see something of others. Nations figure by comparison" (quoted in Black, p. 294). The clearest statement of this viewpoint is (perhaps to some people surprisingly) in a poem by Rudyard Kipling: "And what should they know of England who only England know?" (Kipling, 1891, p. 181).

In practice, the comparisons are usually simplistic, involving *crude stereotypes of national character* applied to the particular cultures. Just occasionally, there is a more sophisticated approach, like the passage in E. M. Forster's

Notes on the English Character (1920, p. 7) in which a dangerous near-accident in the Alps gives the author pause to speculate on the differences between the French and the English, given their very different reactions in what was a hair-raising situation. On the other hand, much of the travel writing and many of the guidebooks simply trot out the clichés one after the other. For example, for William Lee (around 1753) the Germans were "in general"

> a good natured people, hospitable and generous, lovers of pomp and magnificence. I would not look for French vivacity, Italian cunning or English good sense amongst them. Take them as you find them and a traveller may pass his time very well amongst them. I speak of the German nation in general (quoted in Black, p. 64 f.).

F. L. Bevan (1849), the lady missionary whom we have already encountered, was primarily impressed by the hardworking nature of the Germans. Her book is full of catalogue-like lists, in which the different European nations are directly compared and contrasted. Thus the Germans are the most hardworking, the Portuguese the laziest; the Dutch are the cleanest nation, the Poles the dirtiest (p. 88 f.). Two World Wars later, British "experts on Germany" reached slightly different conclusions when they were invited by Margaret Thatcher in 1990 to attend a seminar at the Prime Minister's official country residence, Chequers. The discussions were supposed to remain secret, but reports that were leaked into the media revealed the unflattering statements that had been tabled for the meeting about such German characteristics as

> their insensitivity to the feelings of others [...] their obsession with themselves, a strong inclination to self-pity, and a longing to be liked [... their] angst, aggressiveness, assertiveness, bullying, egotism, inferiority complex, sentimentality [...] capacity for excess, kicking over the traces (Parsons, *No guns*).

148

"National character" does indeed tend to be changeable. The Germans were once seen as dreamy poets and philosophers (Madame de Staël, 1810), in contrast to the warlike French; less than a century and a half later, they were thuggish militarists, crushing the amiable Gallic hedonists with ruthless Teutonic efficiency; most recently (at least in the view of some of the "Anglo-Saxons") they have become timid pacifists.

Even superficial behaviour can change quite spectacularly. As Dr. Samuel Johnson (1773) succinctly noted, "[...] all works which describe manners, require notes in sixty or seventy years, or less" (Boswell, vol. 2). In modern times, the English have become known for their reserve and formality, and for the "Anglo-Saxon touch taboo", but the great Humanist Erasmus (1499) wrote from England to his friend Faustus Andrelinus praising the widespread English custom of *kissing*:

> [...] did you but know the blessings of Britain, you would clap your wings to your feet, and run hither [...] To take one attraction out of many; there are nymphs here with divine favours [...] Besides, there is a fashion which cannot be commended enough. Wherever you go, you are received on all hands with kisses; when you take leave, you are dismissed with kisses. If you go back, your salutes are returned to you. When a visit is paid, the first act of hospitality is a kiss, and when guests depart, the same entertainment is repeated; wherever a meeting takes place, there is kissing in abundance; in fact, whatever way you turn, you are never without it. Oh Faustus, if you had once tasted how sweet and fragrant those kisses are, you would indeed wish to be a traveller. Not for ten years [...] but for your whole life in England (Epistle 98, p. 203).

English kissing behaviour changed quickly. In 1751, a British traveller in Germany, Lord Dartmouth, complained of the social obligation to kiss all the ladies at a dinner party. He did his duty like a man, but not without some reluctance; the weather was hot, and it was sad clammy work. The novelty of the thing surprised me, and the indecency of it shocked me; however agreeable it might prove in particular cases, I never wish to see the custom prevail in England (quoted in Black, p. 63).

A further way of experiencing the Other is to *(deliberately) not experience the Other*. Many people are so assured of the superiority of their own culture that they never bother to leave it. A German acquaintance of mine, from the tiny provincial town of Sarstedt, when asked why she didn't go abroad for her holiday, replied: "Why should I? Everything that I need from life is available here in Sarstedt!" But even those who *do* travel can avoid most contact with the alien culture by doing what many tourists and business travellers do, which is to stay within a safe "culture bubble" of services – familiar, "international" cuisine, a comfortable, Western-style hotel room, airport transfers in an air conditioned bus or taxi, sex with experienced, English-speaking professionals – in other words, protected from contamination by the local culture, which they can nevertheless observe in comfort as if from behind thick bullet-proof glass.

There have always been travellers of this sort – in 1842, the Countess of Blessington expressed her impatience with her fellow countrymen and countrywomen: "It would appear that they travel not so much for the purpose of studying the manners of other lands as for that of establishing and displaying their own" (Withey, 1997, p. 92).

But the phenomenon has increased considerably since the middle of the nineteenth century, as such developments as improvements in transport infrastructure and the spread of organised group travel ("tours") made recreational travelling more accessible to people from relatively lowly social classes. The tourist was not a traveller: one was passive, the other active. "Instead of [remaining] an athletic exercise, travel became a spectator sport" (Boorstin, 1962, p. 93). Paul Fussell (1980), in his study of British literary travellers in the period between the World Wars, distinguishes between *explorers*, who travel in search of the unknown, *travellers*, who travel in areas familiar to them from historical or cultural accounts, and *tourists*, who undertake travel that has been arranged and organised for them commercially (p. 39). This period may have been the last Golden Age of Travel, as adventurous writers penetrated to different parts of Africa or Asia. But it would be wrong to see travel and tourism as being diametrically opposed to each other. Mass tourism copies some of the routes pioneered by "individualist" travellers, there is "adventure travel" organised for groups, and elitist travellers are under constant pressure to find new challenges, which usually remain exclusive only for a short time – thus, for example, the once dangerous overland route from Western Europe to India had become a standard minibus trip for hippies by the Seventies (Withey, p. xi), although it has since become more dangerous once again.

None of these different approaches really makes allowance for the possibility that the Other may be radically *different* from ourselves, though without having to play the role of opposite or reverse image, without being exploited by us solely for purposes of our own, and without being simply a projection of our fantasies; or that it is not necessarily *inferior* to us (this is based partly on Todorov, 1982.)

How should we then behave in our dealings with the strangers and foreigners whom we meet when travelling, and how can we best understand them? The unfamiliar can only be comprehended intelligently in terms of categories that are familiar to us. The act of description (*report*) presupposes a distance between observer and observed that hinders empathetic understanding (*rapport*), whereas the latter requires a denial or suspension of one's own culture and values – what in colonial times was known as *going native*. It is unclear how this problem can be resolved. Even the professionals in this field, the anthropologists, are stuck at this point, since the most important empirical method in their discipline, *participant observation*, is itself a contradiction in terms. How can cultural insights be achieved within the *one* culture and then comprehensibly formulated for the *other*, except by a constant switching of identities, repeated metamorphoses which call the fieldworker's cultural identity into question and put his or her mental stability under tremendous strain?

Numerous anthropologists and cultural theorists have tackled the problem – James Clifford, Hans Peter Duerr, Clifford Geertz, Michel Leiris and George E. Marcus, to name just a few (see also Jarman, 1998, p. 19 f.) – but the puzzle has no obvious solution.

Because of the transient nature of travel, cultural code-switching is slightly easier for travellers, especially for those who are in possession of a wide repertoire of cultural roles and competences and who have the ability to slip temporarily into someone else's skin. People with a *mixed cultural identity* are often very skilled at this. They are "Janus figures", able to comprehend two or more cultures, with empathy or with critical distance, though never simultaneously from different perspectives (in that respect they are like the tricky Gestalt pictures which show you either a vase or two faces, but never both images at the same time).

Charles-Joseph, Prince de Ligne (1735-1814), who was a diplomat, a soldier and a writer, was just such a "Janus figure": "I like my condition of being everywhere a foreigner [*J'aime mon état d'etranger partout*]; French in Austria, Austrian in France, both in Russia, it is the way of enjoying yourself everywhere and so being dependent nowhere" (quoted in Mansel, 2003, p. 46). Ligne even went so far as to appear before the Polish Diet, the Sejm, to beg them (in Latin) to allow him to become a naturalised Pole – yet another nationality! "I come from several different countries at the same time," he told them. "I want to be of yours!" (p. 91) And they agreed.

But even people like Ligne were sometimes forced to choose between their cultures, when, for instance, these happened to be at war with each other. To take a more modern example: Walt Disney's politically correct remake of the classic Western *The Alamo* (2004), in the original version a nationalist saga of American heroism in the face of invasion from Mexico, was subjected to massive criticism, including the comment by film-reviewer Harry Knowles that "You can tell the story of the Alamo from the Mexican or the Texan side. But you can't do both at the same time. You have no one to root for" (quoted in Goodwin, 2003).

If the values of two cultures stand in direct opposition to each other – whether in such matters as political freedoms, the separation of church and state, the treatment of animals, the proper bringing up of children, or the rights of women – it is difficult to know how to behave. Faced with cultural behaviour that offends against your deepest-held values and beliefs, the catchphrase "When in Rome do as the Romans do" will be of little help to you, and, as the literary traveller Tobias Smollett (1776) noted more than two centuries ago, albeit in the fairly harmless context of eating and toilet manners: "There is nothing so vile or repugnant to nature, but you may plead prescription for it, in the customs of some nation or other" (p. 34). Smollett proves his point with some (to our taste) unspeakable examples:

> [...] a native of Legiboli will not taste his fish till it is quite putrefied: the civilized inhabitants of Kamschatka get drunk with the urine of their guests, whom they have already intoxicated: the Nova Zemblans make merry on train-oil: the Groenlanders eat in the same dish with their dogs: the Caffres, at the Cape of Good Hope, piss upon those whom they delight to honour, and feast upon a sheep's intestines with their contents, as the greatest dainty that can be presented [etc.] (*ibid.*).

Even liberal, multicultural societies cannot afford to tolerate all the forms of cultural behaviour practised by all their cultural minorities, if only because some of these will directly conflict with each other; compromises will need to be made, and in the final resort the values of the dominant, majority culture will have to be taken as the yardstick for determining what is acceptable behaviour

A final point needs to be made. Although a traveller probably has the option, in such a difficult conflict situation, to pack his bags and move on, processes of *globalisation* increasingly bring us together with foreigners, whether physically, through economic migration or tourism, or virtually, through such media as the Internet. Opportunities arise, but so do obligations. North Americans and Western Europeans are usually on the stronger side in intercultural encounters: "Those of us who are part of the privileged elite whose lives are being enriched by the processes of globalisation must never forget just how precarious and dangerous the world is for most people" (Altman, 2001, p. 164). The synergetic possibilities of interculturality in international business communication have frequently been noted (see, for example, Jarman, 2001, p. 5 f.), but that is also true in areas like leisure. To be sure, there is a widespread resentment that globalisation may be leading worldwide in the direction of an Anglo-Saxon, "McDonaldized" cultural standardisation (for "McDonaldization", see Ritzer, 1983), but one could also say that it is precisely globalisation that is encouraging processes of cultural syncretisation and making people more aware of the alternatives presented by other cultures. We are being offered opportunities for synergy and self-development, since "[cultural] difference simultaneously challenges and dances with desire" (Weeks, 2002, p. 29).

REFERENCES

Altman, Dennis. *Global Sex*. Chicago: University of Chicago Press, 2001.

Anonymous [Bevan, F. L.] (1849). *Near Home; or, Europe Described*. "Fifth Edition, carefully revised." London: Longmans, Green, 1894.

Beneke, Jürgen. Conversation with the author, April 5, 2004.

Black, Jeremy (1992). *The Grand Tour in the Eighteenth Century*. London: Sandpiper, 1999.

Boorstin, Daniel J. (1962). *The Image; or, What Happened to the American Dream*. Harmondsworth: Penguin, 1963.

[Boswell, James]. *Boswell's Life of Johnson*. Edited by George Birkbeck Hill. Gutenberg Project, Web pages, Vol. 2: The Life of Samuel Johnson, LL.D. (November, 1765-March, 1776), <http://www.gutenberg.org/dirs/etext05/7jhn210.txt>; Vol. 3: The Life of Samuel Johnson, LL.D.

(March, 1776-October, 1780), <http://www.gutenberg.org/dirs/etext 05/7jhn310.txt> (Accessed 29.11.2004)

Casson, Lionel (1974). *Travel in the Ancient World.* Baltimore, MD & London: Johns Hopkins University Press, 1994.

[Erasmus]. *The Epistles of Erasmus from His Earliest Letters to His Fiftieth Year.* Trans. Francis Morgan Nichols (1901). Volume 1. New York: Russell & Russell, 1962.

Forster, E. M. (1920). "Notes on the English Character." In: *Abinger Harvest* (1936). London: Edward Arnold, 1940, p. 3-14.

Fussell, Paul (1980). *Abroad: British Literary Traveling Between the Wars.* Oxford: Oxford University Press, 1982.

Goodwin, Christopher. "It's Crockett the Coward of the Alamo." In: *The Sunday Times*, 9.11.2003, 1, p. 29.

Homer. *The Odyssey, Books 13-24.* Trans. A. T. Murray, rev. by George E. Dimock. Cambridge, MA & London: Harvard University Press, 1995.

Jarman, Francis. *The Perception of Asia: Japan and the West.* Hildesheim: Hildesheim University Press, 1998.

— . SMEs and Intercultural Communication. In: *CultureScan,* 1/3, 2001, Web page, <http://www.culturescan.de/beitraegeD.htm#3j> (22.11.2004)

Johnson, Paul (1972). *The Offshore Islanders: England's People from Roman Occupation to the Present.* Harmondsworth: Penguin, 1975.

Kipling, Rudyard (1891). "The English Flag." In: *The Complete Verse.* London: Kyle Cathie, 1990, p. 181-183.

Lenček, Lena/Bosker, Gideon (1998). *The Beach: The History of Paradise on Earth.* New York: Penguin Putnam, 1999.

Loti, Pierre [pseudonym of Louis Marie Julien Viaud] (1887). *Japan [Madame Chrysanthème].* Trans. Laura Ensor. London: T. Werner Laurie, [1915].

Mansel, Philip. *Prince of Europe: The Life of Charles-Joseph de Ligne, 1735-1814.* London: Weidenfeld & Nicolson, 2003.

Obermann, Constanze. *Empathie und Emotion im interkulturellen Gespräch.* Unpublished M.A. thesis, University of Hildesheim, 2003.

O'Rourke, P. J. "Seoul Brothers." In: *Rolling Stone,* 11.2.1988, p. 93 f., 98, 100 f., 118.

Outhwaite, William. *Toward a European Civil Society?* Web page,<http://www.zmk.uni-freiburg.de/Online_Texts/outhwaite_european_civil_society.htm> (18.04.2004)

Parsons, Anthony. *No Guns for the Huns!: Anti-German Feeling and Post-War German Rearmament.* Web page, <http://www.univ-pau.fr/~parsons/antigerm.html> (22.11.2004)

Plutarch. *The Rise and Fall of Athens: Nine Greek Lives.* Trans. Ian Scott-Kilvert. Harmondsworth: Penguin, 1960.

RE = *Paulys Realencyclopädie der classischen Altertumswissenschaft. 42: Polemon to Pontanene.* Munich: Alfred Druckenmüller, 1952.

Rhodes, Cecil (1877). *Confession of Faith.* Web page, <http://husky1.stmarys.ca/~wmills/rhodes_confession.html> (24.11.2004)

Ritzer, George. "The McDonaldization of Society." In: *Journal of American Culture,* 6, 1983, p. 100-107.

Smollett, Tobias (1776). *Travels through France and Italy.* Ed. Frank Felsenstein. Oxford: Oxford University Press, 1981.

Staël, Germaine de [Madame de Staël] (1810). *Über Deutschland [De l'Allemagne].* Trans. Friedrich Buchholz *et al.* Frankfurt/M.: Insel, 1985.

Tacitus. *Agricola, Germania, Dialogus.* Cambridge, MA: Harvard University Press, 1970.

Theroux, Paul. *The Great Railway Bazaar: By Train Through Asia.* London: Hamish Hamilton, 1975.

Thorpe, D. R. *Selwyn Lloyd.* London: Jonathan Cape, 1989.

Todorov, Tzvetan (1982). *The Conquest of America: The Question of the Other [La Conquête de l'Amérique].* Trans. Richard Howard. New York: Harper Colophon, 1985.

Weeks, Jeffrey. "Bangkok – the New Vienna." In: *The Times Higher Education Supplement,* 1.3.2002, p. 28 f.

Withey, Lynne (1997). *Grand Tours and Cook's Tours: A History of Leisure Travel, 1750 to 1915*. London: Aurum, 1998.

IX.

ALEXANDRIA: THE INVENTED CITY

In his introduction to an English translation of a modern Egyptian novel, John Fowles, the British novelist, had this to say about its romantic setting, Alexandria:

> Open cities are the mothers of open societies, and their existence is especially essential to literature – which is why, I suppose, we cherish our illusions about them, and forgive them so many of their sins. In the case of Alexandria, that prototype cosmopolis and melter of antitheses, we can hardly be blamed. *Antony and Cleopatra*, Cavafy, E. M. Forster, Lawrence Durrell...there is a formidably distinguished list of foreign celebrants and from them we have taken an indelible image of the place. It is languorous, subtle, perverse, eternally *fin de siècle*; failure haunts it, yet a failure of such richness that it is a kind of victory (1978, p. vii).

"An indelible image" – even though this is an Alexandria that probably never existed or, if it did, only very briefly.

There have been many cities, countries even, which genuinely never existed, other than in literature or in the fantasies of adventurers and explorers. They become the focus of our dreams and fears, and enable these to take on a shape and a name: Eldorado; Shangri-La; Atlantis; Mordor. And there are also those geographical names – like Alexandria – which, although they refer to real places, have a resonance that is connected more with the faded glories of the past or with the yearnings of poets than with any modern significance that the places may have: Timbuctoo; Mandalay (where Kipling's "flying fishes play"); Samarkand; Tahiti. But whether they are real places turned to some more poetic purpose, or merely fictional creations, we have an emotional need for such symbolic landscapes.

Many years ago I had a friend who was a municipal employee in a small provincial town in Germany. As a hobby he studied international railway timetables (those were days when international air travel in Europe was very expensive and quite unusual). He dreamt of a great journey of escape – to Bari in Italy. Why Bari of all places? Why not Rome, Naples, Florence or Venice? Rome, Florence and Venice were too familiar: they had already been worked to death in art and writing, and all four cities were well-known to him from television. Bari, on the other hand, was almost completely unfamiliar, but it could – just – be reached by train, and without too many complicated connections. Also – and this was crucial – it was a *port*. In other words, it was border country, a place that offered a possible opening to other worlds and to unfamiliar experiences. Bari was his existential Plan B, the notional ticket in his pocket for the day when, just before the leaden grey sky of middle-aged boredom and routine crushed down on him, he would make his getaway. The knowledge that an escape route was available to him was part of his mental hygiene. Bari itself meant nothing to my friend, and actually going there would no doubt have been a deflating, depressing experience, yet the *idea* of Bari played a significant and useful role in his life.

The Egyptian city of Alexandria has been a powerful symbolic force in the modern literary imagination. Twentieth-century readers yearned for something that they envisioned and called "Alexandria". Ever since it was founded, this peculiar and unnatural city has enabled writing that could not have been created without it, even though most of the writers lived there as exiles or were temporary visitors. Many of those who came to Alexandria never belonged to it, but were expatriates and outsiders. They and the city were metaphors of each other, because, almost until the present day, Alexandria was in Egypt but not truly part of it.

COMING TO ALEXANDRIA

The Alexandria of the imagination remains ephemeral, most bitterly for those who come to the city with expectations fuelled by romantic longings. As the American novelist Thomas Pynchon (1963) puts it, via his character Aïeul, a "café waiter and amateur libertine" (p. 63):

How wrong to expect any romance or sudden love from Alexandria. No tourists' city gave that gift lightly. It took – how long had be been away from the Midi? twelve years? – at least that long. Let them be deceived into thinking the city something more than what their Baedekers said it was: a Pharos long gone to earthquake and the sea; picturesque but faceless Arabs; monuments, tombs, modern hotels. A false and bastard city [...] (p. 64).

First impressions of Alexandria could be deeply disappointing. Joachim Sartorius, author of a recent anthology of writings about Alexandria (2001), found it, on his first visit, "huge and broken-down", "dirty and dusty and hot and in the end unbearable. There were only stones, and the wide circle of eclectic constructions with orangey-white facades on the Corniche, and the dirty sea" (p. 12 f.). Back in 1768, the traveller James Bruce had also noticed the "ill-imagined, ill-constructed, and imperfect buildings" and was quite eager to leave the city (Sattin, 1988, p. 10 f.); Edward Lane in 1833 had described Alexandria as dirty (p. 71); and Florence Nightingale (1849) had made the observation: "There is nothing in Alexandria but the [Main] Square and the huts of the Alexandrians" (p. 155). She found Alexandria too European and cosmopolitan (p. 83 f.).

Flaubert, a very different kind of traveller, arrived in Alexandria in the same week as Florence Nightingale. After the initial turbulent impact of Africa – "I gulped down a whole bellyful of colours, like a donkey filling himself with hay" (Flaubert, p. 29) – he reached much the same conclusion about the city as Nightingale. "Alexandria is almost a European city", he complained in a letter to his mother, although in his quest for exotic excitement he was already spotting promising details, like the naked breasts of some of the local women or a procession celebrating the circumcision of the son of a rich merchant (*ibid.*).

For most visitors, the attractions of Alexandria were not self-evident; in the view of a British civil servant, Ronald Storrs, who lived and worked there before the First World War, "Alexandria is not an obvious city; she requires, before revealing herself, time, study and love" (Sattin, p. 163). But Alexandria has a powerful legend, which exerts far more influence on the imagination than anything that is actually *there*. This legend is based on two phases in its history, the first of them – which provided inspiration and material for some of the writers of the second phase – beginning with the foundation of the city by Alexander the Great.

THE ANCIENT CITY

Wherever he went, Alexander established new cities named after himself. Alexandria in Egypt was one of many Alexandrias, although it became the greatest of them. Rather than remaining just a fragile Greek colony planted on hostile soil, under the dynasty of the Ptolemies its population was soon an exciting, confused mixture of Greeks, Egyptians, and Jews, the greatest cultural and commercial centre of the ancient world, and, until Alexandria was overtaken by Rome, its largest urban centre. This artificial city was given its own deity, Sarapis, the only god ever created by a committee. King Ptolemy I Soter was (supposedly) told in a dream to fetch a statue from distant Pontus on the Black Sea which "would cause the kingdom to prosper"; "whatever place gave the image shelter would become great and famous" (Tacitus, p. 264). Egyptian priests and Greek advisors were consulted. The wonderful statue was indeed found (surprise, surprise) and brought to Egypt, and a huge temple was built to house the new cult. Like his city, Sarapis (*Illustration 5*) was a compound of different elements – from Egypt, the god Osiris and Apis, the sacred bull, and from Greece the divinities Zeus, Hades, god of the underworld, Aesculapius, god of healing, and Dionysus, god of mysteries and of wine.

When Ptolemy and his son Ptolemy II Philadelphus founded a "Museum", or research institute, and a great library, they made Alexandria the most important centre of learning in the ancient world, but once again the essential element had to be imported – the scholars and poets were mostly exiles or "braindrain" expatriates rather than native Alexandrians. Zenodotus, the first librarian, came from Ephesus; Eratosthenes, renowned for his accurate calculation

of the circumference of the earth, came from Cyrene, as did
the famous poet Callimachus, who pioneered library cata-
loguing; Aristophanes, not the Athenian playwright of that
name but a renowned textual scholar and a pioneer of punc-
tuation, was from Byzantium; Aristarchus, who edited
Homer, came from Samothrace; Theocritus, the great bucolic
poet, was from Syracuse in Sicily.

Illustration 5: Sarapis – the invented god (on a bronze coin of
Alexandria struck in 149/150 A.D.).

The huge library of Alexandria accumulated all the known wisdom of the world, an effort not really attempted again until the French *Encyclopédie* of the eighteenth century and only today being achieved, perhaps, in the form of the World Wide Web. To accomplish this, the Alexandrians had to be ruthless. Ships entering the harbour of Alexandria were required to give up any manuscripts they had on board and take copies instead. The official Athenian copy of the works of the three great tragedians, Aeschylus, Sophocles, and Euripides was retained by forfeiting the enormous deposit of fifteen talents that had been pledged for its return to Athens (Griffin, 1996, p. 9). The Alexandrians could substantially hinder the activities of other libraries, like that of Pergamon, by their virtual monopoly of the supply of papyrus, and they were not over-scrupulous in their relations with such rivals. One of the charges levelled against Mark Antony by his enemies with regard to his behaviour towards Cleopatra was that in order to please her the lovesick Roman ordered 200,000 volumes from the Pergamene library to be sent to Alexandria (Plutarch, p. 271; Plutarch does note that "most of the charges thus brought [...] were thought to be falsehoods", but he was writing more than a century after the event, and at the time someone clearly thought that large-scale library piracy was something that the Alexandrians were perfectly capable of stooping to).

ALEXANDRIAN LITERATURE

During the third century B.C. and until the middle of the second, Alexandria was the literary capital of the Greek world, but Alexandrian literature was a "literature of exhaustion" (Fordyce, p. 37). The Alexandrian poets were, according to F. L. Lucas (1951),

> painfully conscious of living in the lengthening shadow cast by giant predecessors. They are heirs to great wealth, yet they feel impoverished; they are more cultured than their fathers, yet more sterile; their shelves teem with books, their heads with knowledge, yet they lack the old passion, energy, and life. For

when the past becomes more than the future, memories [more] than hopes, then a man – or a race – is growing old (p. 119).

The poetry of the Alexandrians is elegant rather than energetic. Here, for example, the most renowned of the poets, Callimachus, elegises another poet, Heraclitus of Halicarnassus (in the exquisite, though free, nineteenth-century translation by William Johnson Cory) – *Nightingales* was the title of a book by Heraclitus:

They told me, Heraclitus, they told me you were dead,
They brought me bitter news to bear and bitter tears to
    shed.
I wept as I remember'd how often you and I
Had tired the sun with talking and sent him down the
    sky.
And now that thou art lying, my dear old Carian guest,
A handful of grey ashes, long, long ago at rest,
Still are thy pleasant voices, thy *Nightingales*, awake;
For Death, he taketh all away, but them he cannot take.

The heroic age of Greece was over. Callimachus, who produced mostly shorter works, had a famous quarrel with his pupil Apollonius of Rhodes on the question of the appropriateness of epic poetry in the traditional manner, and was generally held to have won the argument. But if the old greatness could no longer be achieved, three things still remained – "the decorative surface of the universe, the delights of study, and the delights of love" (Forster, 1922, p. 32). The poetry became ornate, full of learned mythological references, and love was a principal theme. There was no great *Alexandrian* past to remember, but the poems could be set in mythological locations or amidst the pastoral scenery of Sicily. Only a few poems, such as Theocritus's "Fifteenth Idyll", present a view of everyday Alexandrian life; more often, shepherds and rustic folk discuss their loves in a setting much more like Sicily than like urban Alexandria or the villages of the Nile delta. Indeed, in the introductory poem to his *Idylls*, Theocritus directly reminds the reader that he is a Syracusan (*The Greek Anthology*, IX, p. 434).

THE DECADENT CITY

Egypt was a rich treasure for its Roman conquerors, but difficult to handle. The province of Egypt, a vital source of grain for the Roman proletariat and the gateway to trade with India and the East, was too important to be treated just like any other conquered territory, and so it was given a governor with special status, a Prefect who was under the direct control of the emperor. Egypt formed a separate trading zone, with strict customs controls and its own currency, which was valid only within the province. Alexandria was the greatest trading and cultural centre of the Roman world. It was perhaps also the most fascinating city of the empire, with one of the Seven Wonders of the World – the Pharos lighthouse – as well as the Museum and the great Library, but also shops, nightclubs, and superb music (see Casson, 1974, p. 258 f.). For wealthy Roman visitors, it was the starting point for tourist excursions up the Nile to Memphis, the Pyramids, and the Colossus of Memnon.

Among Romans, the moral reputation of Alexandria was distinctly dubious. Juvenal uses it as a touchstone for vice in his "Sixth Satire" when he writes:

When that senator's wife, Eppia, eloped with her fancy
   swordsman
To the land of the Nile, the Alexandrian stews,
Egypt itself cried out at Rome's monstrous morals
   (p.130).

Alexandria became and has remained legendary for its richness and decadence, which found their culmination in the almost mythical figure of Cleopatra VII, the last of the Ptolemies. The historical personage, an intelligent rather than attractive woman who played dangerous power games (and ultimately lost), has been irretrievably transformed into the siren or sex goddess who seduced first Julius Caesar and then Mark Antony. Cleopatra is the embodiment of Eastern sensu-

166

ality; as Antony admits in Shakespeare's *Antony and Cleopatra*, "the beds i' th' east are soft" (Act II, Scene 6, l.50).

In addition to the many plays, novels and films about Cleopatra herself, there have also been lush fictional accounts of life in Alexandria, notably Pierre Louÿs's bestseller *Aphrodite* (1896). Louÿs, an aesthete who corresponded with Oscar Wilde and was a friend of Gide and Valéry, produced voluptuous writings that were very much to the *fin de siècle* taste. A recent comment on these works – "Louÿs's refined evocations, not to say re-inventions, of the society of Hellenistic Greece proved extremely popular in both France and the English speaking world, especially due to [their] somewhat risqué nature" (Web page) – is a considerable understatement. The overwrought style of *Aphrodite* homologises with the panting sensuality of its subject matter. Queen Berenice, for example, is described as being

> clothed in a shamelessly openwork costume which has been fashioned before her eyes by a courtesan from Phrygia. This costume exposed the skin at the twenty-two places where caresses are irresistible, so that even if one exhausted the wildest dreams of amorous fancy during a whole night, there would be no need to remove it (p. 39).

Then there are dancing girls:

> Their dancing was voluptuous, languorous, and without any apparent pattern [...] Soon they formed into couples, and without pausing in their dance, unknotted their girdles and let their pink tunics fall to the floor. A scent of naked women spread around the men, stronger than the perfume of the flowers and the smell of the half-eaten meats. They leant backwards with abrupt movements, pushing out their bellies and holding their arms over their eyes. Then, hollowing out their loins, they straightened up, and their bodies touched with the tips of their shaking breasts. Timon felt his hand caressed by a warm, fleeting thigh (p.129).

The lovemaking of two women is described:

> They don't embrace each other, but simply brush together to taste ecstasy. [...] Human love is only distinguished from the stupid rutting of animals by two divine practices: the caress and the kiss. And it is women who deserve the credit here, for it is they who have perfected them (p. 99, 100).

According to one of the male characters, the "supreme mission of woman" is "[To] prostitute herself, with or without art" (p. 130), and there are numerous descriptions of sensual situations.

Aphrodite may be no more than a steamy nineteenth-century projection of personal fantasies, but it seems also to draw on Roman erotic texts like the *Letters of Courtesans* of Alciphron and the *Erotic Letters* of Aristainetus. Though these are set – with conventional anachronism – in Classical Athens, and not known to be connected with Alexandria, they reflect the style and manners of the hedonistic Roman East. One of Alciphron's courtesans describes a party:

> [...] since we were a bit tipsy our thoughts turned to – you know what I mean. We stroked the hands of our lovers, gently unbending their flexed fingers, and between cups we engaged in amorous sport. One and another lay back and kissed her lover, letting him feel her breasts; and as if she were turning away she would actually press her hips on his groin. And now our passions were rising, and there was a rising [*no comment!*] among the men too [...] (p. 289, 291).

In another letter, there is a "beautiful bottom competition" between two of the courtesans (p. 297 f.) that might have graced *Aphrodite*. Judging by writings like these, and by the evidence specific to Roman Egypt collected by Dominic Montserrat (1996), we can easily reach the conclusion that, even without the embellishments of Pierre Louÿs, the real Alexandria of the late first century B.C. and of Roman times may well have been a lively place. Or, as Robert Flacelière

(1960) puts it in his assessment of Louÿs' novel: "The book is too artificial and exaggerated to pass as a realistic picture of its subject. But the general impression it leaves is not altogether misleading" (p. 134).

Alexandria was also a turbulent city, with tensions between its different ethnic groups, between Christians and pagans, and then between the various Christian sects. When the Arabs finally conquered the city, in 642, they seem to have been uncertain what to do with it. The victorious Muslim general, Amr, reported to the Caliph that he had taken "a city of [...] 4,000 palaces, 4,000 baths, 400 theatres, 1,200 greengrocers and 40,000 Jews" (Forster, 1922, p. 61 f.), but nevertheless the Arabs preferred to build their own city inland at Fustat, which was later to become Cairo.

BRITISH ALEXANDRIA

The second phase in the legend of Alexandria begins in the nineteenth century. Under Turkish viceroys of the Ottoman sultans, Egypt was effectively independent, but it was also an object of interest for the French and the British. The Khedive Ismail (1863-79) spent vast amounts on prestige construction projects and luxuries, culminating in the building of the Suez Canal (1869). After he had ruined the country Britain stepped in. The British took control of the Canal and then established their rule over the whole of Egypt, first as a "veiled protectorate" and later, when a later Khedive made the mistake of appointing a pro-German prime minister during the First World War, as a formal British Protectorate (December 1918).

Alexandria was now a booming Levantine trading metropolis trapped between Europe and the Middle East, but belonging to neither, and (as in ancient times) full of Greeks, Italians and other non-Egyptian groups. The atmosphere in the city was quite different to that in Cairo.

Officially, as well as commercially, Alexandria was nearer to Europe than Cairo; and, remarkably for those old Islamic days, the repos hebdomadaire [weekly closing day] was kept, both in the city and on

169

the quays, not as elsewhere on [the Muslim] Friday, but on the Christian Sunday (Ronald Storrs, quoted in Saad el Din & Cromer, 1991, p. 195).

Alexandria had a large commercial population of non-Egyptians. The Anglo-Egyptian humorist "Rameses" (in reality, Major C. S. Jarvis, C.M.G., O.B.E.) refers to them as "Greek grocers" (Jarvis, 1937, p. 33), and describes them as a useful category of person because of their tendency to "die for England's sake"; as he explains,

they are always murdered when [an Egyptian] mob turns anti-British. The reasons for this are, firstly they are much easier to kill than Englishmen, they are more plentiful, their shops are well worth looting, and everybody owes them money (p. 3).

It was with the non-Egyptians – though not exclusively with grocers, of course – that many of Alexandria's writer-exiles spent their time. When the writer Robert Graves was considering applying for a university teaching post in Egypt, his friend T. E. Lawrence ("Lawrence of Arabia") wrote to encourage him, pointing out that, with regard to the Egyptians, "you need not dwell among them. Indeed, it will be a miracle if an Englishman can get to know them" (Graves, 1929, p. 264).

Social contacts with other Europeans were very important because of the sheer strangeness of North Africa. Robin Fedden, who spent the Second World War years in Egypt, described after his return to Britain how "exhausting" the cultural isolation of exile could be for writers:

It is possible to travel almost anywhere in Europe without getting quite off a familiar cultural beat; whatever the country, Christianity – whether the inhabitants like it or not – is at the back of the way they think and act. Once you cross to Islamic Africa it is a different story; nothing is to be taken for granted, and you don't even know the general shape and outline of things (quoted in Saad el Din & Cromer, 1991, p. 92).

170

Alexandria was full of colourful and unusual people. They were far more interesting than the "sights" of the city. Visitors like Hector Dinning, an Australian soldier of the First World War wounded at Gallipoli and brought to Alexandria to convalesce, discovered "the secret to sight-seeing in Alexandria", which is that

> there are few monuments to visit and the museum [...] is small, so consequently there is little that the sightseer is compelled to do. He has the time to sit and watch the Alexandrians. [And] Dinning had the impression that there was little for them to do, either, since the cafés always seemed to be full and the people he watched encouraged the idea that they, too, had no work to do. Perhaps nowhere else in the world had [Dinning] encountered such a serious and lasting enjoyment of idleness (Sattin, p. 171).

E. M. FORSTER

Among those who looked after soldiers like Dinning was the English novelist E. M. Forster, who arrived in Alexandria in 1915 as a Red Cross volunteer and stayed for three years. Forster was not always enthusiastic about the city itself – "I am weary beyond expression of Alexandria, its trams and its streets. One is as far from the East here as in London. All is so colourless and banal" (letter to S. R. Masood, September 8, 1917, in *Selected Letters*, I, p. 269) – but he came to know the city very well and wrote two books about it: *Alexandria: A History and a Guide* (1922), and a collection of short pieces, *Pharos and Pharillon* (1923). Although he wrote no major work of fiction about Alexandria, the city was hugely important in Forster's life in several ways.

For example, it was here that he fell in love, with an Egyptian tram-conductor, Mohammed el Adl, and at the age of thirty-nine had his first full sexual experience. He is, incidentally, the only one of Alexandria's major literary celebrants who "formed an important relationship with an Egyptian – of either sex" (Michael Haag, in Forster, 1922, p.264). Although Forster was very English, he found it easier to express some ideas or feelings that were important to him, for example sexual tolerance, through reference to a non-English Other. His relationship with Mohammed el Adl enabled him to establish human trust "across the barriers of income race and class" (letter to Florence Barger, July 18, 1917, *Letters*, I, p. 263). And he uses Alexandria itself as a metaphor, a symbolic stage of transition to India, the subject of his greatest novel, *A Passage to India* (1924):

> The Mediterranean is the human norm. When men leave that exquisite lake, whether through the Bosphorus or the Pillars of Hercules, they approach the monstrous and extraordinary; and the southern exit leads to the strangest experience of all (p. 270 f.).

Alexandria, with its Greek/Arab mix, marked the border between Europe and the disturbing but also exciting world beyond, an idea that reoccurs in other writers on Alexandria and which is parodied by V. S. Naipaul in that writer's own "passage to India", *An Area of Darkness* (1964): "here," he writes in his description of disembarking from the liner at Alexandria, "and not in Greece, the East began: in this chaos of uneconomical movement, the self-stimulated din, the sudden feeling of insecurity, the conviction that all men were not brothers and that luggage was in danger" (p.10).

CONSTANTINE P. CAVAFY

Forster had another important encounter while he was in Egypt, with the great Alexandrian poet Constantine P. Cavafy. Other well-known poets have been associated with Alexandria, for instance the Italians Filippo Tommaso Marinetti and Giuseppe Ungaretti, both of whom were born there, but Cavafy is so much part of the legend of Alexandria that Durrell can refer to him in the *Quartet* simply as the "poet of the city" (p. 30 *et passim*). Forster (1923) describes him, famously, as "a Greek gentleman in a straw hat, standing absolutely motionless at a slight angle to the universe" (p.91), a description that captures Cavafy's gentle eccentricity but perhaps also reflects back onto Forster's feelings about his own homosexuality. In addition, it could be taken to describe the cosmopolitan Alexandrians themselves, at first recognisably Greek, Italian, British, Jewish, or Armenian but, then again, *not quite*. And it helps to explain why writers may have felt exiled in Alexandria, not belonging, but at the same time at home there, with a distance (or an "angle"!) to their subject matter, and a richly rewarding social and literary subsoil in which to work

"Slight angle" is a massive understatement. Cavafy's poems "deny, ridicule, or (worst of all) ignore the three bulwarks of respectable bourgeois society: Christianity, patriotism, and heterosexual love" (Bien, 1964, p. 4), which must have made him immediately appealing to Forster, who set no store by *any* of these things. Forster can be given credit for publicising Cavafy's work internationally and arranging for translations into English to be made. Cavafy himself had gone to school in England, was more or less bilingual, reportedly spoke Greek with a slight English accent and supposedly even "thought" his poems in English (Furbank, 1978, p. 31 and footnote). He published very little during his lifetime, but circulated the poems among his friends. He lived alone in a flat at 10, Lepsius Street, in an area known for its prostitutes, and produced some intensely personal poetry, though not so much explicit descriptions of the sexual act as postcoital or nostalgic musings like the following:

Return often and take me,
beloved sensation, return and take me –
[...] when the lips and the skin remember,
and the hands feel as if they touch again [...]
(from "Return", 1912, *The Complete Poems*, p. 43).

For most of his poems, however, Cavafy, who was a Greek of the Diaspora, favoured historical themes. His subjects were taken not from the Golden Age of Greece, but from periods or settings of decline and decadence: the Hellenistic kingdoms that followed the death of Alexander; obscure frontier outposts of Greek civilisation; the late Roman period, with Christianity pushing out the ancient religion; and Byzantium. To Cavafy (as, likewise, to Forster, who was

173

allergic to muscular empire-builders), periods of civilised decline were more attractive than those of self-confident, aggressive expansion. Peter Bien (1964) has suggested that Cavafy used the history of Alexandria and of the Hellenistic and Byzantine worlds as analogues of his own psychological, economic, and social condition (p. 31), which could well be described as one of decadence, frustration, and decline. Cavafy remained a petty official of the Ministry of Irrigation and showed little interest in contemporary culture or in the lives of Alexandria's Arab population (his lovers, whose services he probably paid for, were young Greeks, not Egyptians).

Cavafy distils poetry from historical missed opportunities, from casual encounters, and from memories. Alexandria is the framework for several of his historical poems – a multicultural enclave, cut off from the rest of the world, onto which he could project his ironic historical vision from the perspective of an outsider.

His Alexandria is a city of the imagination, a "remembered" or "felt" city, not a real one. With great sensitivity he could draw together in a poem the strands of personal feeling and the historical moment. In "The God Forsakes Antony" (1911), for example, he recounts a famous incident reported by Plutarch (as Shakespeare also did, in *Antony and Cleopatra,* Act IV, Scene 3), but turns it into a meditation on the artificiality and transience of the human situation:

> When suddenly at the midnight hour
> an invisible troupe is heard passing
> with exquisite music, with shouts –
> do not mourn in vain your fortune failing you now,
> your works that have failed, the plans of your life
> that have all turned out to be illusions.
> As if long prepared for this, as if courageous,
> bid her farewell, the Alexandria that is leaving [...]
> (*The Complete Poems*, p. 30).

Life for Cavafy was completely identified with Alexandria; to lose the one was to lose the other. In another, much later, poem, "In the Same Space" (1929), he refers to the neighbourhoods that he has known for years, then adds: "I have created you in joy and in sorrows: / Out of so many circumstances, out of so many things. / You have become all feeling for me" (*The Complete Poems*, p. 158). At the end of his life, and dying of cancer, he was invited to come to Athens, but refused: "Mohammed Aly Square is my aunt. Rue Cherif Pacha is my first cousin, and the Rue de Ramleh my second. How can I leave them?" (Leontis, 2001, web page).

LAWRENCE DURRELL

Just as E. M. Forster had found himself in Alexandria during the First World War, two other great novelists of the century served with the Allied forces in Alexandria during the Second World War. The Australian Patrick White observed the goings on in the city with a distinctly cynical eye:

Alexandria during those war years must have been at its most frivolous, its most corrupt. The glitter of its diamonds was betrayed by its values, which were never more than paste. There was usually a motive behind its hospitality and woozy kindness: to marry off a daughter to an English Honourable, or better still a warrant-officer with solid middle-class civilian prospects, or simply to fuck the troops, or clinch a swill contract with the Camp Commandant. Most of us loved this eclectic whore of the Near East, her pseudo-French and Breetish [*sic*] pretensions, her Jewish warmth, her Greek loyalty and realism. Silken, boring Alexandria, pinned between the desert and the sea, with no outlet but adultery and bridge (1981, p. 91).

Like Forster before him, White was not inspired to write a major novel about Alexandria, but, just as Forster did, he found in Alexandria the great love of his life, an Egyptian Greek named Manoly Lascaris.

Lawrence Durrell is the modern writer whose name is perhaps most often associated with Alexandria. Durrell came to Egypt in 1941 and worked as a war time Press Officer for the British Information Office in Cairo before being transferred to a similar job in Alexandria. Like Forster and White, he also began a great affair there. In general, he was overwhelmed by the beauty of the women in Alexandria. As he wrote in May 1944 to his friend the novelist Henry Miller:

> [...] Alexandria is, after Hollywood, fuller of beautiful women than any place else. Incomparably more beautiful than Athens or Paris; the mixture Coptic, Jewish, Syrian, Egyptian, Moroccan, Spanish gives you slant dark eyes, olive freckled skin, hawk-lips and noses [sic], and a temperament like a bomb. Sexual provender of quality [...] (*The Durrell-Miller Letters*, p. 171. The "sexual provender" assertion is repeated in the *Quartet*, p. 17; all page references are to the slightly revised one-volume edition).

Durrell had already met a particularly interesting woman, Eve ("Gipsy") Cohen, who was to become the muse of his famous *Alexandria Quartet*:

> [...] a strange, smashing, dark-eyed woman I found here last year, with every response right: every gesture; and the interior style of a real person – but completely at sea here in this morass of venality and money. The only person I have been able to talk to really; we share a kind of refugee life. She sits for hours on the bed and serves me up experience raw – sex life of Arabs, perversions, circumcision, hashish, sweetmeats, removal of the clitoris, cruelty, murder. As a barefoot child of Tunisian Jewish parents, mother Greek from Smyrna, father Jew from Carthage, she has seen the inside of Egypt to the last rotten dung-blown flap of obscenity. She is [Miller's erotic novel] *Tropic of Capricorn* walking. Her experiences as a child here would make one's hair stand on end (p. 169 f.).

Eve Cohen clearly provided much of the exotic material for the *Quartet*, and the first volume, *Justine* (1957), is dedicated to her.

The *Alexandria Quartet* is a difficult work, complex in its plot structure, confusing in the ways that its numerous characters mesh with each other, and lush and sometimes obscure in its style. As Durrell himself explains, the first three books, *Justine*, *Balthazar* (1958) and *Mountolive* (1958), are "intercalary", relating to each other as "siblings" rather than "sequels" (p. 7). They operate in space rather than in time, in the sense that they cover similar plot material but approach the events from different perspectives; new revelations require a reassessment of what has already been learnt and create a constant knock-on effect with regard to the inter-related feelings and motives of the characters. The final novel, *Clea* (1960), however, "was intended to be a true sequel and to unleash the time dimension. The whole was intended as a challenge to the serial form of the conventional novel: the time-saturated novel of the day" (*ibid.*). In the words of the critic G. S. Fraser (1968/1973), who was also in Egypt during the war and knew Durrell well:

> The whole of *The Alexandria Quartet* is an archaeological excavation of motives, in which it is difficult to get down to the layer below without destroying the layer we are at, and in which the very bottom layer is perhaps never reached at all (p. 121).

Taken altogether, the *Quartet* is a complex study of the different types of love and of the interplay between men and women. On the simplest level, it is a *Bildungsroman* of the would-be writer Darley – an Irishman (p. 38; Durrell's mother was Irish), who is not actually *named* until p. 356! – who moves to maturity and to being able to write through a series of relationships with women: Melissa, Justine, and Clea. To achieve his goal he must give up Alexandria. He escapes to a Greek island, but realises: "I must return to [Alexandria] once more in order to be able to leave it forever, to shed it" (p. 659), and the very last words of the *Quartet* are "Vision is exorcism" (p. 881).

He must also give up Justine, who in a series of shifting equations is identified with *all* women, Love, the Goddess or Female Principle, and the city of Alexandria itself.

Thus: Justine is "not really a woman but the incarnation of Woman" (p. 61). According to Clea, she "verges on the Goddess" (p. 68). Balthazar, the gossipy homosexual doctor who lives in Cavafy's Lepsius Street, says that "all our women are Justines [...] in different styles" (p. 81). She is "a child of the city" (p. 44). "A city becomes a world when one loves one of its inhabitants" (p. 57; the idea is repeated on p.832). Alexandria is "the great winepress of love" (p. 18). The city itself is a love-trap: "Justine would say that we had been trapped in the projection of a will too powerful and too deliberate to be human – the gravitational field which Alexandria threw down about those it had chosen as its exemplars..." (p. 22).

The Goddess was worshipped in ancient times as a triad, of virgin or nymph (Artemis; the waxing moon), mature woman (Aphrodite; the full moon), and mother or crone (Hera, Demeter, Hecate; the waning moon). Aphrodite is the goddess of Love, and is associated in the *Quartet* both with Alexandria and with Justine. She is a tyrant who demands complete obedience and gives no guarantee that she will provide something in return. One of the key statements of the *Quartet* is: "One learns nothing from those who return our love" (p. 674). Aphrodite is referred to directly several times, her name coupled with adjectives like "austere", "merciless", "mindless", "primeval" and "primitive" (p. 89, 92, 558). We are told about "the cataract with which Aphrodite seals up the sick eyes of lovers, the thick, opaque form of a sacred sightlessness" (p. 241): Love is blind.

The Justine of the first novel is ruthless Aphrodite: she is selfish and sexually dangerous – "I think this Jewish fox has eaten my life", her husband complains (p. 130). But looking for her lost child in the children's brothel (p. 41-43), Justine is also Demeter, the mother searching for her lost daughter Persephone in the Underworld. And as the apparent victim of incest-rape (p. 69), she is Artemis the virgin. (So is Darley's pathetic, fragile girlfriend Melissa, whose surname is "Artemis" and whose first name means "bee" – the bee was an important symbol at Ephesus, where there was a great cult of Artemis.) "Nymph? Goddess? Vampire?" Justine is "all of these and none of them" (p. 694), because the Goddess, despite her different aspects, is essentially indivisible.

178

"Read as a single, independent work, *Justine* might well stand as the most intensely romantic novel of the twentieth century" (Koger, web page), mainly because of the way in which the besotted poet Darley refracts everything that he experiences, including Alexandria, through the unreliable prism of his obsession with Justine. But in the course of the later novels

> the intensely poetic romance surrounding Justine herself, presiding presence of the first, most frequently read book, is [...] exposed as a charade of deceptions, with the *femme fatale* finally a predator. The depths were all shallows (Turner, 1998, web page).

In *Balthazar*, the cynical Pursewarden describes her as "a tiresome old sexual turnstile through which presumably we must all pass" (p. 285). From being the irresistible Cleopatra who conquered Caesar and Antony she has become the ageing schemer rejected by the cold-blooded Octavian. Justine loses her mythical status and stands revealed as humanly fallible, superficial and opportunistic, yet she also becomes more interesting as a person. As a "real person" she can also be complex and multi-faceted, and one could even imagine a further set of intercalary novels constructed around her – Durrell had indeed speculated that "even if the group of books were extended indefinitely the result would never become *roman fleuve*" (p. 7).

SEX, VIOLENCE AND PURPLE PROSE

The Alexandria of Durrell's *Quartet* is flashy, exotic, and grotesque, a city of whores, lepers and eunuchs, in which people have horrific physical deformities or terrible diseases like smallpox or lupus, torture, blind or murder each other, hack off hands, crack whips, and constantly seduce each other. As a place to read about rather than live in, it could be seen as a fantasy world for people who have not quite grown up. "And when you were twenty," writes Sartorius (2001), "didn't you too devour the *Quartet*, your eyes moist and red with yearning for distant lands?" (p. 11). It is very un-British! Durrell was never really part of the literary "scene" in Britain, and in any case chose to spend almost all of his life abroad. The escapist elements that, back in the Fifties and Sixties, gave the *Quartet* much of its appeal to readers in grey, rainy Britain – the exaggerated cruelties, the hedonistic wallowing in sex, the shouts, screams and colours of an exciting city – also excluded Durrell from the literary mainstream of the time. One reviewer who knew Alexandria very well, D. J. Enright, subjected the *Quartet* to an considerable roasting: "His characters can't have a drink in the Place Zagloul without 'in the room above a poor wretch screaming with meningitis' [...] Nessim's 'great house' is patrolled by 'black slaves': call them 'servants' and how the glory dims!" (1968, p. 45). "Perhaps it is in a desperate attempt to endow his creations with character that Durrell deprives them of limbs" (p. 46). Or, referring to the intensified plot focus, later in the *Quartet*, on political conspiracy: "By this time the best-disposed of Durrell's readers, I should have thought, would welcome any sort of intrigue *not* amorous" (p. 51). And so on.

Enright's own novel set in Alexandria, *Academic Year* (1955), is principally about the melancholy lives of expatriates at the fag end of the Empire, when a British passport wasn't "as young and virile as it used to be" (p. 219). Enright shows more interest in his Egyptian characters than Durrell, but the Alexandrian background – of poverty, riots, and general unease – is depressingly realistic. Yet although Enright doesn't romanticise sex and violence, they are both there: Packet, the central figure of the novel, has an affair with Sylvie, "a rather attractive Syrian girl" (p. 56), and another British character is knifed to death by Egyptian villagers. Both events would have seemed very exotic to most British readers in the 1950s.

The sensuality and the violence that Enright admits and Durrell wallows in were part of the legend of Alexandria, but also part of its reality. Memoirs and letters (including Durrell's) make it plain that there was plenty "going on" in Alexandria in the Forties, and much of it would have been exotically new to young men from Britain. During both world wars, British and Australian military personnel were "serviced" in the brothels of Alexandria. One famous establishment was known as "Combakir", "not as one might imagine a Turkish word, but the soldiers' interpretation of the last seductive call of the girls as they left the house: 'When you're in town again, come back 'ere'" (Mostyn, 1989, p. 146). Given Durrell's friendship with Henry Miller and the robust nature of his early novel *The Black Book* (1938; in a preface to a later edition Durrell himself referred to its "crudity and savagery", p. 10), perhaps the most surprising thing about the *Quartet* is that, barring one or two briefly glimpsed couplings, there are no actual sex scenes.

The cruelty which is so obvious an element in the *Quartet* may seem to be exotic, nightmare stuff, but much of it is realistically grounded in the brutality of life in a poor, Middle Eastern city. It also echoes the bizarre, well-remembered cruelties of the Turkish rulers of Egypt in the nineteenth century: a singer fails to give satisfaction because she has a cold, and her tongue is torn out (Mostyn, 1989, p.32); a slave girl falls asleep while on duty, and her mistress orders her pot of tea to be boiled on a charcoal fire lit between the girl's breasts (p. 30); women are stitched into sacks filled with rats and thrown into the Nile (p. 38); a princess drives through the streets in her carriage, selecting young men to be brought to the palace to pleasure her but be murdered afterwards (p. 47 f.). This is the tradition within which Durrell places the sinister figure of Memlik Pasha, Minister of the Interior, around whom "[legends] collect easily":

"Once when he was threatened by impotence he went down to the prison and ordered two girls to be flogged to death before his eyes while a third was obliged" – how picturesque are the poetical figures of the Prophet's tongue – "to refresh his lagging spirits" (*Quartet*, p. 601).

However, the two most vividly described scenes of cruelty in the novels involve the butchering alive of camels (p. 56, 488). It may not have been necessary for Durrell to invent cameos like these: those who have travelled in poorer parts of Asia and Africa will know that extreme brutality towards animals is not a rare occurrence.

The lush, often "purple" style of the *Quartet* is high-risk writing without a safety net, and it stands in contrast to other British novels of the time, many of which have a tendency towards moral earnestness, stylistic caution and provinciality. The descriptive writing in the *Quartet* is often magnificent:

> In autumn the female bays turn to uneasy phosphorus and after the long chafing days of dust one feels the first palpitations of the autumn, like the wings of a butterfly fluttering to unwrap themselves. [Lake] Mareotis turns lemon-mauve and its muddy flanks are starred by sheets of radiant anemones, growing through the quickened plaster-mud of the shore (p. 43).

In the city itself there is the "clang of the trams shuddering in their metal veins as they pierce the iodine-coloured *meidan* of Mazarita" (p. 18), the Syrians "going to bed with little cries, like migrating birds" (p. 60), or "a prostitute singing in the harsh chipped accents of the land to the gulp and spank of a finger-drum" (p. 318).

But the language is evocative not of Alexandria but of "Alexandria". The descriptions are not realistic, but poetic or magical, they

> do not evoke [...] one street in Alexandria as seen by Darley at one particular time. They are patterned from a multiplicity of facets, profiles, or inflexions, and thus seem, while graphic in their vividness, to carry a weight of heraldic or emblematic meaning (Fraser, 1968/1973, p. 116, paraphrasing remarks made in a B.B.C. radio talk by the poet Christopher Middleton in 1957).

From the safe distance of his Greek island, Darley, whose voice we hear in these descriptions, is engaged in an activity not unlike Cavafy's: he is "creating a city of remembered experience" (Robillard, 1981, p. 80).

182

In addition to the shorter passages, there are also great poetic set-pieces like the following, taken from the early pages of *Justine*:

In that early spring dawn
With its dense dew
Sketched upon the silence which engulfs a whole city
Before the birds awaken it
I caught the sweet voice
Of the blind *muezzin* from the mosque
Reciting the *Ebed*
A voice hanging like a hair
In the palm-cooled upper airs
Of Alexandria:
"I praise the perfection of God
The Forever-Existing"
(This repeated thrice, ever more slowly,
In a high sweet register)
"The perfection of God, the Desired, the Existing,
The Single, the Supreme:
The perfection of God, the One, the Sole,
The perfection of Him
Who taketh unto himself no male or female partner
Nor any like Him
Nor any that is disobedient
Nor any deputy, equal or offspring.
His perfection be extolled"
The great prayer wound its way
Into my sleepy consciousness
Like a serpent,
Coil after shining coil of words
(The voice of the *muezzin* sinking
From register to register of gravity)
Until
The whole morning seemed dense
With its marvellous healing powers
The intimations of a grace
Undeserved and unexpected
Impregnating
That shabby room where Melissa lay

Breathing as lightly as a gull
Rocked
Upon the oceanic splendours
Of a language she would never know (p. 27).

I have set it out here as a poem because it *is* a poem, but it appears in the text as continuous prose.

ALEXANDRIA TODAY

Today Alexandria has been reclaimed from the writers, exiles and expatriates by the people of Egypt. In his novel *Miramar* (1967), the great Egyptian novelist Naguib Mahfouz, the first Arabic winner of the Nobel Prize for Literature (1988), describes how the Egyptian Amer returns to stay once again at the Pension Miramar. He tries to reassure the ageing Greek landlady Mariana that Egypt is her home, and that "there's no place like Alexandria":

"Monsieur Amer, I don't know how you can say there's no place like Alexandria. It's all changed. The streets nowadays are infested with *canaille*."
"My dear, it had to be claimed by its people." I try to comfort her and she retorts sharply.
"But *we* created it" (p. 6).

Alexandria was created not only by its people, but by the writers who brought it to life. Now, that Alexandria has gone, leaving only memories and echoes, or, as Naguib Mahfouz so poetically formulates it, a "Core of nostalgia steeped in honey and tears" (p. 1).

REFERENCES

Alciphron. "Letters of Courtesans." In: *The Letters of Alciphron, Aelian and Philostratus*. Trans. Allen Rogers Benner & Francis H. Forbes. Cambridge, MA/London: Harvard University Press, 1949, p. 250-341.

Aristainetus. *Erotische Briefe*. Trans. Albin Lesky. Zürich: Artemis, 1951.

Bien, Peter. *Constantine Cavafy*. New York & London: Columbia University Press, 1964.

Callimachus. "Heraclitus." Trans. William Johnson Cory. In: *The Faber Book of Epigrams and Epitaphs*. Ed. Geoffrey Grigson. London: Faber, 1977, p. 183.

Casson, Lionel (1974). *Travel in the Ancient World*. Baltimore, MD: Johns Hopkins University Press, 1994.

Cavafy, C. P. [Konstantinos Kavafis] *The Complete Poems*. Trans. Rae Dalven. London: Hogarth Press, 1961.

Durrell, Lawrence (1938). *The Black Book*. Including a preface by the author written in 1959. London: Faber & Faber, 1977.

—. *The Alexandria Quartet*. Consisting of *Justine* (1957), *Balthazar* (1958), *Mountolive* (1958) and *Clea* (1960). One-volume edition, slightly revised (1962). London: Faber & Faber, 1968.

— "Henry Miller." *The Durrell-Miller Letters, 1935-80*. Ed. Ian S. MacNiven. London: Faber/Michael Haag, 1988.

Enright, D. J. (1955). *Academic Year: A Novel*. London: Buchan & Enright, 1984.

—. "Alexandrian Nights' Entertainment." In: *Writing in England Today: The Last Fifteen Years*. Ed. Karl Miller. Harmondsworth: Penguin, 1968, p. 45-53.

Flacelière, Robert (1960). *Love in Ancient Greece* [*L'Amour en Grèce*]. Trans. James Cleugh. London: Frederick Muller, 1962.

Flaubert, Gustave. *Flaubert in Egypt: A Sensibility on Tour*. Ed. and Trans. Francis Steegmuller. Chicago, IL: Academy, 1979.

Fordyce, C. J. "Latin Alexandrianism." In: *The Oxford Classical Dictionary*. Ed. M. Cary *et al*. Oxford: Oxford University Press, 1949, p. 36 f.

Forster, E. M. (1922). *Alexandria: A History and a Guide*. With Notes by Michael Haag. London: Michael Haag, 1982.

— (1923). *Pharos and Pharillon*. London: Michael Haag, 1983.

— (1924). *A Passage to India*. London: Book Club Associates, 1987.

— *Selected Letters of E. M. Forster, Volume One, 1879-1920*. Ed. Mary Lago & P. N. Furbank. London: Collins, 1983.

Fowles, John. "Introduction," in *Naguib Mahfouz* (1967), p. vii-xv.

Fraser, G. S. (1968). *Lawrence Durrell: A Study*. Revised edition. London: Faber & Faber, 1973.

Furbank, P. N. (1977). *E. M. Forster: A Life*. New York & London: Harcourt Brace Jovanovich, 1978.

Graves, Robert (1929). *Goodbye to All That*. Rev. ed. Harmondsworth: Penguin, 1960.

The Greek Anthology. Trans. W. R. Paton. Vol. III. Cambridge, MA/London: Harvard University Press/Heinemann, 1917.

Griffin, Jasper (1996). "The Library of Our Dreams." In: *Pro Europa: Athenaeum*. Web page, <http://iggi.Unesco.or.kr/web/iggidocs/01/952647950.pdf> (24.09.2004)

Juvenal. *The Sixteen Satires*. Trans. Peter Green. Harmondsworth: Penguin, 1967.

Koger, Grove. "The Alexandria Quartet." In: *The Literary Encyclopaedia*. Web page, <http://www.litencyc.com/php/sworks.php?rec=true&UID=10820> (9.10.2004)

Leontis, Artemis. "Cavafy's World." In: *Kelsey Museum Newsletter*, Fall 2001. Web page,<http://www.lsa.umich.edu/kelsey/research/Publications/fall2001/cavafy.html>(8.10.2004)

Louÿs, Pierre (1896). *Aphrodite*. Trans. Robert Baldick. London: Panther, 1972.

Lucas, F. L. (1951) *Greek Poetry*. London: Dent, 1966.

Mahfouz, Naguib (1967). *Miramar*. Trans. Fatma Moussa-Mahmoud. London/Cairo: Heinemann/The American University in Cairo, 1978.

Montserrat, Dominic. *Sex and Society in Graeco-Roman Egypt*. London & New York: Kegan Paul International, 1996.

Mostyn, Trevor. *Egypt's Belle Epoque: Cairo, 1869-1952*. London & New York: Quartet, 1989.

Naipaul, V. S. (1964). *An Area of Darkness*. Harmondsworth: Penguin, 1968.

"Pierre Louÿs, 1870-1925." Web page, <http:// www. kalin.lm.com/louys.html> (25.09.2004)

Plutarch. "Antony." In: *Plutarch's Lives*. Trans. Bernadotte Perrin.Vol. IX. Cambridge, MA/London: Harvard University Press/Heinemann, 1920, p. 137-333.

Pynchon, Thomas (1963) *V*. London: Picador, 1975.

"Rameses" [Major C. S. Jarvis, C.M.G., O.B.E.]. *Oriental Spotlight*. With illustrations by "Roly". London: John Murray, 1937.

Robillard, Jr., Douglas. "In the Capital of Memory: The Alexandria of Durrell and Cavafy." In: *On Miracle Ground: Proceedings of the First National Lawrence Durrell Conference*, April 25, 1980. Ed. Michael Cartwright. *Deus Loci: The Lawrence Durrell Newsletter*, special issue 1, vol. V, Fall 1981, p. 78-87.

Saad el Din, Mursi/Cromer, John. *Under Egypt's Spell: The Influence of Egypt on Writers in English from the 18th Century*. London: Bellew, 1991.

Sartorius, Joachim (Ed.). *Alexandria – Fata Morgana*. Stuttgart & Munich: Deutsche Verlags-Anstalt, 2001.

Sattin, Anthony. *Lifting the Veil: British Society in Egypt, 1768-1956*. London: Dent, 1988.

Shakespeare, William. *Antony and Cleopatra*. In: *The Complete Works*. Ed. Peter Alexander. London & Glasgow: Collins, 1951, p. 1155-96.

Tacitus. *The Histories*. Trans. Kenneth Wellesley. Harmondsworth: Penguin, 1964.

Turner, Martin. *Lawrence Durrell and the* Alexandria Quartet. May 12, 1998. Web page, < http://www.50connect. co.uk/turner/criticism/criticismLD01.html> (9.10.2004)

White, Patrick. *Flaws in the Glass: A Self-Portrait*. London: Jonathan Cape, 1981.

X.

WRITING ABOUT EVIL

I learned that evil is a reality, not an abstraction
of moral philosophy, and that the killers of innocent
people must be held responsible or evil will prevail
(John Shattuck, 2003, p. 7 f.)

Why do writers of fiction write what they do? There are lots of reasons, and the reasons may be as different from each other as people can be different. Some writers, for example, write for money, to earn a living, become rich, or, like Walter Scott, pay off their debts; some have a yearning to be admired or to become famous; some write as a civilised, educational hobby or as a way of passing the time in a gracious and interesting manner; some write because they see that as their profession, and, like V. S. Naipaul, have never done anything else; for some, writing is an intellectual exercise, or a challenge; or a personal therapy; some are *driven*, writing manically through the night after a long day's work in the office; for others, writing is a by-product of the work that they do in their full-time job as a journalist or academic; some write because a friend encourages them; or because there is an opportunity for their book to be published or their play performed; some write to leave a memorial of themselves to their children; some write because they have something to prove to the world, or just to one single, very important, person; or because they love their language, and can't *not* write; or because there is something that they are burning to say; or because certain emotions would otherwise overwhelm them; or because the Muse or the White Goddess or the Holy Spirit compels them; some writers write to take shelter from the real world in a world of their own, or to create a personal mythology; or they write just for fun.

Some of these reasons are true for things that I've written, but I am going to take the Fifth Amendment on this – with one exception. *A Star Fell* (1998), my first play for the stage – actually, my second, though the first to be performed

– was created out of a deep sense of frustration and helplessness. I wrote the play in the summer of 1997. Two years earlier, in what had once been Yugoslavia, Bosnian Serb troops commanded by General Ratko Mladić had overrun the so-called "safe area" of Srebrenica; an estimated 7,414 Bosnian Muslim men and boys were taken away and subsequently murdered. I was indignant about this, but unable to express my feelings.

Why did I react so strongly to the events in Srebrenica? I had no Yugoslav relatives or close friends, and I had never even been to Yugoslavia, except for one occasion when, as a student, I had travelled the length of the country by train on my way back from Greece. Srebrenica may have been "the worst atrocity in Europe since the Second World War" (this was the tag that was quickly attached to it in the Western European media), but there were far more terrible things going on in the world, for instance in Rwanda. Here, in just one hundred days in 1994, at a killing rate "five times that of the Nazi death camps" (Shawcross, 2000, p. 104), 800,000 or more Tutsis and moderate Hutus were murdered by Hutu soldiers, policemen and villagers. To the resentment of Africans in particular, little attention was paid to Rwanda, either by the media or the world powers, who were focused on what was happening in the Balkans. When the Secretary-General of the United Nations, Boutros Boutros-Ghali, asked the Clinton administration to jam the hateful broadcasts of the Hutu extremist radio station Mille Collines, he was told (he says) that it would be too expensive (p. 119; see also Shattuck, p. 38 f.). There was something of a general feeling among Westerners that there were *always* problems in Africa, and that not too much by way of energy or resources needed be diverted towards dealing with them – an attitude which might help to explain the waspish remark made by (the African) Boutros-Ghali to the desperate, beleaguered citizens of Sarajevo that they had "a situation that [was] better than ten other places in the world" (Shawcross, p. 204).

The horrors in Rwanda should have made us more indignant, but Srebrenica was so much closer. When, some years later, Bill Clinton explained on television the reasons for NATO military intervention in another Balkan crisis, in

190

Kosovo, he said that Kosovo was important because *it was only an hour away from where Americans went on vacation* (p. 324). That closeness made all the difference. For Western Europeans, living in a continent that is a patchwork of fairly small states, Bosnia was just a few frontiers away; some people had even driven there, on their way to Athens or Istanbul. In addition to that, Bosnia was in *Europe*. Things like that were not supposed to happen here: we were tolerant, progressive and multicultural, we had exorcised our demons in 1945, and even the end of Communism had been (almost) bloodless and painless.

I wanted to write something about the dreadful mess that led to the Srebrenica Massacre, though not as a factual account. Books like that had already been published (*e.g.*, Honig & Both, 1996; Rohde, 1997), and the sequence of events was more or less clear.

SREBRENICA

Within so-called "safe areas", supposedly under the protection of the United Nations, Bosnian Muslims waited in 1995 to be attacked by Serb forces. No governments were eager to commit large numbers of ground troops. U.N. forces were therefore inadequate to protect the Muslims, though if they tried to move them out to safety they were accused of collaborating with the Serbs in the "ethnic cleansing" of Muslim areas. Under Security Council Resolution 836 (June 1993), the U.N. role was defined as one of "deterring attacks" against the safe areas, rather than defending them, and although UNPROFOR (the United Nations Protection Force) was authorised in the event of attacks to take all necessary measures, including the use of force, Britain, France and Spain insisted on the words "acting in self-defence" being inserted into the text. These attacks became more likely because of the murderous guerrilla raids launched by Muslim commanders like Naser Orić from within the shelter of the safe areas. The Muslims' own Sarajevo government exploited the increasingly desperate position of the enclaves to put moral and political pressure on the international community. When the final attack on Srebrenica came, the U.N.'s cumbersome chain of command failed, and there were no air strikes until it was too late. In response, the Serbs threatened to kill their Dutch prisoners if the strikes continued. Their gamble paid off – no one in a command position, whether military or political, in the U.N., UNPROFOR, NATO or the Dutch government, showed the nerve to stand up to these threats. The air strikes were called off, and soon afterwards the Dutch troops, demoralised and intimidated by the heavier fire-power of the Serbs, could only stand by as Muslim men and boys were taken away. What happened next was described by a judge at the International Criminal Tribunal at The Hague, Fouad Riad:

> After Srebrenica fell to besieging Serb forces in July 1995, a truly terrible massacre of the Muslim population appears to have taken place. The evidence tendered by the prosecutor describes scenes of unimaginable savagery: thousands of men executed and buried in mass graves, hundreds of men buried alive, men and women mutilated and slaughtered, children killed before their mothers' eyes, a grandfather forced to eat the liver of his own grandson. These are truly scenes from hell, written on the darkest pages of human history (quoted in Shawcross, p.139; see also Judah, 1997, p. 239 f.).

The international powers have no cause to be proud of their role in all this. The crisis had been triggered in June 1991 by Croatia's secession from the Yugoslav federation, "discouraged by the United States but encouraged by Germany, its traditional ally" (Shawcross, p. 43; Serbs were still bitterly aware of the German-Croat connection during the Second World War). In December, the European Union announced that it would recognise the breakaway republics of Croatia and Slovenia under certain conditions; Germany declared that it would do so anyway (p. 48). If Germany favoured the Croats, the Russians tended to support the Serbian government of Slobodan Milošević, and the United States the Bosnian Muslims, yet none of the major nations showed any willingness to provide the extra manpower needed for effective peace-keeping (let alone peace-*enforcement*). The French at the last moment came up with a hare-brained scheme for their troops to be flown into Srebrenica in U.S. helicopters (Shattuck, p. 153). The United States, remembering the quagmire of Vietnam and paralysed by the deaths of eighteen U.S. soldiers in Somalia, called for tougher action against the Serbs but refused to back up the rhetoric with American ground forces. In July 1991 Secretary of State James Baker had told the press, "We have no dog in that fight" (p. 317); later, General Colin Powell explained, "We do deserts, we don't do mountains" (Steyn, 1999).

Then there are the more obvious villains of the story, notably the Serbian puppet master Milošević, the weird Bosnian Serb political leader Radovan Karadžić (a psychiatrist, nationalist poet, and author of children's books), and, above all, the clownish but sinister Ratko Mladić. Mladić strutted in front of his troops, bullied the Dutch peacekeepers and "magnanimously" offered the helpless Muslims his protection – "Allah can't help you now. But Mladić can" (Rohde, p. 189) – even as the massacre was getting under way. At the sight of the prisoners, he reportedly said to his soldiers, "There are so many! It's going to be a feast [*mezze*]. There will be blood up to your knees" (Shawcross, p. 145). Yet behind the vengeful glee with which the Serbs tortured, beat, shot, and mutilated their captives there was a cold-blooded calculation. In the struggle for control of Bosnia, the Serbs were thinly stretched and at a demographic disadvantage to the Muslims – here was a heaven-sent opportunity to readjust the manpower ratio by taking out 7,000 Muslim males in one go.

So much for the *events* of Srebrenica. But I wanted to fathom *emotionally* how it could have happened, who had caused it and perhaps even how such horrors might be prevented in future. I had learnt from writers like Ivo Andrić and Rebecca West how complex the cultural-historical mix in the Balkans was, and I was very aware that I knew almost nothing about the region first-hand. I knew somewhat more about India – I had Indian friends, I had travelled fairly extensively there, I had done the reading and I had taught university classes on India and on the British Raj. Most importantly, I felt an *empathy* with India. I was less likely to make a complete fool of myself (I hoped!) if I wrote about India than if I wrote about the Balkans. And there was an Indian massacre, too, that was as vile and complex as the massacre in Srebrenica.

CAWNPORE

In the course of what in Britain is called the Great Indian Mutiny, native Indian troops on June 27, 1857, massacred hundreds of British soldiers and civilians who had been besieged in the garrison town of Cawnpore but then given safe-conduct to evacuate down the Ganges to Allahabad – they were suddenly attacked without warning as they embarked in the boats provided for them; later, in a second massacre on July 15, there was a slaughter of more than two hundred prisoners, mostly women and children, who had been spared in the first killing. The bodies of the victims of the second massacre were thrown down a well, which afterwards became a memorial (*Illustration 6*) and which as a tourist site in British India drew even more visitors than the Taj Mahal.

Just as with the accounts of Srebrenica, in reading about these events you soon find yourself asking: How can people who have known each other for so long do such things to each other? And: How is such a massacre "caused"? It isn't enough just to analyse motives and political factors, although that can be done as well. A literary reconstruction offers the chance to explore the interaction of those involved, the interplay of fear, hatred and laziness, the motivation that is sometimes merely opportunism.

A STAR FELL

In some ways, my play *A Star Fell* is a study of the different forms of evil.

There is the straightforward vengefulness of the *Sultana Oula*, the mistress of the Nana Sahib, the Indian petty prince who was nominally in command at Cawnpore.

Illustration 6: "The Memorial Well at Cawnpore", a plate illustration by the Krebs Litho Co., Cincinnati, from George Moerlein, *A Trip Around the World*, Cincinnati, OH: M. & R. Burgheim, 1886.

She forces his hand, manipulating events so as to cause both massacres, and from a hiding-place watches the first massacre with great relish:

> SULTANA OULA. This is a moment I have waited for for many years. Look at them, the proud British! Look at them climbing onto the boats! See how they scramble! Ha! She is fat, that one! No, she is with child! She thinks she is taking her unborn bastard with her! And there is the clerk, the rat, the arrogant one who used to pay over our money! But now he has no trousers! Look at his spindly little legs! And he is bleeding! You British devils, where is your dignity now? *[To* HUSAINEE*]* This is indeed good sport! (p.68)

She finds it easy to hate the British, and has very personal reasons for doing so. It was British so-called "land reforms" which ruined her father, driving him off the land and leading to her and her sister being sold into slavery and (in her case) prostitution.

> SULTANA OULA. And every time that I had to give myself to someone in a dark corner, for a handful of copper coins, every time that I was hired to dance and sing for a drinking party, every time that I was *used*, it was the British that I thought of (p. 80).

But the Sultana has anther motive for what she does – a lust for power. She knows that her source of power is her control over the spineless and indolent Nana Sahib. She must therefore prevent him leaving to join the other mutineers at Delhi, where he would quickly be sidelined by more competent and dynamic leaders, and she must prevent the mutinous soldiers from leaving too. The best way to keep them in Cawnpore is by keeping them occupied there – by launching an attack on the British garrison.

The performance of the actress (Jessica Prentice) who played the Sultana in the original production was a masterly study in seething vindictiveness. She prowled the stage like an Indian tigress, graceful but threatening, spitting out her hatred and (verbally) flashing her claws.

SULTANA OULA. [...] The Nana Sahib is busy with his British friends, may they rot! It will take a long time. "Hughie, shall we play billiards?" "Dondy, that would be so wonderful! Will you come to the polo game this evening? There will only be British officers and their ladies present, no Indians, only the finest society!" "Oh Hughie, that would be absolutely topping! Please, please, let me be your poodle." "Dondy, you are such a well-behaved nigger, I shall ask John Company [*i.e., the British East India Company*] to pay you two rupees more." "Oh Hughie, how generous you are!" May they rot in hell! (p. 47)

Someone who had seen the production spoke to me about it a few weeks later and told me how furious he had been that the Sultana didn't get her deserved comeuppance at the end of the play – instead (as so often happens to such people in real life) the nastiest of the villains got clean away, and with the money too! He had almost wanted to jump up onto the stage and strangle her, he told me (and this is surely the biggest compliment a playwright can ever receive... though it is good that he *didn't* do it).

The Sultana is contrasted with the scheming courtier *Azimullah Khan*, whose spite is weaker because it is more cerebral. He too is fuelled by bitterness and resentment. Although of princely blood, he was brought up by missionaries as a "charity boy"; although he is well aware of his own intelligence and sexual attractiveness, he is also constantly reminded of how his race and skin-colour place oblige him to serve people whom he knows to be humanly inferior to him.

The Sultana tells him that they are "two of a kind" (p.49), but she also realises how different they are: "You hate with the head, I hate with the heart" (p. 78). Unlike her, he takes no personal pleasure in the killings: "I told you that I saw no reason why I should watch the killings. They were necessary. But it's not modern to enjoy watching such things. What will the rest of the world think of us?" (*ibid.*). He re-

197

jects the sadistic offer that she makes regarding the captured British women:

> SULTANA OULA. You are such a ladies' man, Azim. We have a hundred British ladies as our prisoners. [...] I offer you the choice of the prisoners. Pick them... like flowers. Treat them as your garden, Azim.
> AZIMULLAH KHAN. No.
> SULTANA OULA. Why not? This is so unlike you! It could be very amusing. *[laughing]* Think what you could allow yourself to do to the *memsahibs*! Think of the games you could play! (p. 80-81)

She hasn't realised that Azimullah is only interested in breaking the pride of the British, not in enjoying their humiliation (just as a "ladies' man" quickly loses interest in each conquest and moves on to the next one).

The most nationalistically inspired of the Indian characters is the slave-girl *Husainee*, whose patriotism even her mistress the Sultana finds somewhat exaggerated:

> SULTANA OULA. British India will go up in flames.
> HUSAINEE. And out of the ashes we shall create an Indian nation.
> SULTANA OULA. Husainee, you are such an idealist! (p. 83)

There is a cold, political element in Husainee's hatred for the British. This becomes apparent in the scene in which she and the prostitute *Azeezun* humiliate the British women prisoners by setting them degrading menial tasks like sweeping and scrubbing.

> HUSAINEE. Look at the *feringhee* [*i.e., white foreigners*], they have no idea how to work!
> AZEEZUN. Let's play a game with them, let's see which of us can annoy them most! *[To the English ladies]* Look at this! Look at the proud ladies!
> HUSAINEE. We are feeding you, but you must

work for your food!

LADY WHEELER. Sweepers, low-castes bring us food they would not even feed to their animals! Some of the children are dying. Why are you doing this to us?

AZEEZUN [mockingly]. O burra-memsahib, great lady, how does the world look from down there?

MRS. JACOBI [quietly]. You are cruel. We never harmed you.

HUSAINEE. You harmed me with your pride, you harmed me with your arrogance, you harmed me with the colour of your skin!

AZEEZUN kicks MRS. JACOBI so that she falls over.

AZEEZUN. Look at you!

HUSAINEE. Yes, tomorrow I shall bring more people to look at you. It is good that Hindus and Muslims see you like this.

LADY WHEELER. Why do you put us on show like animals?

HUSAINEE. So that my people see you, working in the dust like Untouchables. Look at you now! You will never lord it over us again. And why do you complain? You are still alive. Enjoy your work!

AZEEZUN. I would have put you to work in a house of pleasure, but no man would pay to take you. I told the sweepers, "Do what you like with the burra-memsahib, fuck her if you want to", but they have better women to take the edge off their lust.

HUSAINEE [crushingly]. Go and clean the latrines. You are old and useless and dirty. Clean them with your hands.

LADY WHEELER and MRS. JACOBI exeunt.

AZEEZUN. [...] "Go and clean the latrines." That was nasty!

HUSAINEE. Azeezun, you have a good heart, but why must you speak in such a way, with "shit" and "fuck" and other bad words? Sometimes you speak like a man, like a low-caste. Why do you need to use these words?

AZEEZUN. Oh, that's just me. I don't always mean what I say. I get it from the soldiers. *[She laughs]* I get *lots* of things from the soldiers!

HUSAINEE. Do you mean what you say about the *feringhee*?

AZEEZUN. I don't know. But it's fun, isn't it? They were high up there, *[sneering]* real fine, the lords and ladies, and look at them now!

HUSAINEE. Azeezun, we are doing something truly great. You are playing a small part, but in a great action. Do you realise that?

AZEEZUN. Oh, I suppose so. I don't know. As long as it's fun, eh? Anyway, you won the game, didn't you? "Go and clean the latrines"!

HUSAINEE. Who said anything about a game? I have no time for games (p. 92-95).

Husainee is a hate-filled, puritanical fanatic, while Azeezun is boisterous, thuggish, and "out for a laugh", but both make major contributions to the unfolding of the tragedy.

The traditional villain of the Cawnpore Massacre has always been the *Nana Sahib*, a frustrated princeling who dreams of inheriting the famous title of Peshwa of the Marathas. In *A Star Fell* he is shown – more realistically, I believe, given what we actually know about him – as a pathetic, clownish figure, unable, once the Mutiny has begun, to fill the role of Peshwa that he had so coveted, and carried away by events. He brandishes an enormous sword, but in inappropriate situations, and only his eunuch is impressed (p.59). At the key moments he makes spontaneous decisions but leaves his vague instructions to be implemented by other, more sinister, characters.

NANA SAHIB *[petulently]*. Oh, let the British escape then. I have no quarrel with the British. Nobody plays billiards with me anymore since this started. Now that I am Peshwa, I have no quarrel with them. Send them a message. Let them go to Calcutta. Give them safe conduct. Give them boats (p. 60).

He sleeps through the first massacre, and afterwards, without intending them any harm, unwittingly hands the survivors over to their bitterest enemy:

NANA SAHIB. Prisoners? What prisoners?

AZIMULLAH KHAN. The prisoners in the House of the Women. The women and children whose lives you so graciously spared after the shooting on the riverbank.

SIRDAR KHAN. The wife of General Wheeler is among them.

NANA SAHIB. Oh, poor Wheeler, how sad it was! But who was it who started the shooting? *I* gave no orders. These things happen in war. But I saved the women and children, history will remember me kindly for that, I am sure of it.

AZIMULLAH KHAN. But what should be *done* with the prisoners, Highness?

NANA SAHIB. Done? Who needs to do anything? Let them go *[with a vague flourish of the hand]*, send them to Havelock, get rid of them! Sirdar Khan can organise it. Ah, Wheeler... I miss him sometimes. Nobody here knows how to play billiards properly.

SIRDAR KHAN. Your Highness ordered that the prisoners should be placed in the care of the Sultana.

NANA SAHIB. So I did! And quite right, too, it is better for a woman to deal with these matters of women and children. They have a gentler touch. We rough men have unfinished business on the battlefield and in the conference chamber! *[To* SIRDAR KHAN*]* See that the orders of the Sultana are carried out!

The only character who is an out and out killer is *Sirdar Khan*, yet he is doing no more than "carrying out orders". The *Butcher* who helps him to hack the women and children to death does it for money:

SIRDAR KHAN. You are a butcher?

BUTCHER. Since my childhood, lord. It has been the lowly profession of my family since the beginning of the world.

    SIRDAR KHAN. Then you are well-qualified for the task that I have for you. *[He holds out a purse]* A *well-paid* task.

    BUTCHER *[with mistrust, but taking the purse]*. I won't slaughter pigs.

    SIRDAR KHAN. That will not be required. Do you have your knives with you? *[The* BUTCHER *brings out a set of knives]* Are they sharp?

    BUTCHER. Sharp enough for any animal that I know of (p. 119).

Although both massacres in the play can be shown on stage, the real horror comes across more chillingly in remarks like those of the butcher – firstly, his unwillingness to kill "unclean" pigs (but he *will* kill people), and, secondly, his reply to Sirdar Khan's question about the sharpness of his knives.

    The *British* are nominally the victims, but they have provoked their fate by their arrogance, and by blindly trusting the wrong people at the wrong moment. In several scenes, their failings as rulers before the Mutiny (or their cruelty afterwards) are spelled out.

    SULTANA OULA. [...] there is nothing here but hatred for the British. They have taken away the rights of the princes. They have stolen the farmers' land. They show no respect for temple or mosque. They tell the sepoys to bite on animal fat. And everywhere they go they hold up their heads with arrogant pride and say, "This is *our* land, not yours!" (p. 51).

WRITING ABOUT EVIL

    Are any of the characters in *A Star Fell* "evil" in the sense of being gratuitously vicious? All of them are motivated by easily understandable reasons to perform their cruelties or treacheries (as was probably also the case at Srebrenica). Although "evil" villains abound in fiction, it is hard to find authentic cases in real life, except for deranged psychopaths, as I discovered when I started collecting docu-

202

mentary examples. The Auschwitz doctor and "medical researcher" Dr. Josef Mengele, who forbade a mother, Ruth Elias, to feed her newborn baby in order to observe how long it would take the baby to die without nourishment; the paedophile rapist who kills his victim in order to "cover his tracks"; or the 9/11 pilots who tilted the wings of their aircraft at the last moment so as to "take out" the maximum numbers of floors of the building (Salman Rushdie, 2002, p.437) – they all had their reasons for what they did.

Evil is so terrifying because it is something that we can understand. It comes very close to us. As Prospero admits, at the end of *The Tempest*, "this thing of darkness" – the deformed slave Caliban, who Prospero himself has raised and educated – "I / Acknowledge mine" (Act V, Scene 1, 11. p. 275 f.). Evil can arise in almost everyday situations, out of an unfortunate juxtaposition of circumstances or combination of individuals. We can comprehend it better through the opportunities for empathy and projection offered by literature.

REFERENCES

Andrić, Ivo (1945). *The Bridge on the Drina*. Trans. Lovett F. Edwards. New York: New American Library, 1967.
— . *The Pasha's Concubine and Other Tales*. Trans. Joseph Hitrec. London: George Allen & Unwin, 1969.

Elias, Ruth. *Triumph of Hope: From Theresienstadt and Auschwitz to Israel*. New York: John Wiley & Sons, 1998.

Honig, Jan Willem/Both, Norbert (1996). *Srebrenica: Record of a War Crime*. New York etc.: Penguin, 1997.

Jarman, Francis. *A Star Fell*. Hildesheim: Cambria, 1998. Second edition, Hamburg: Libri, 2000.

Judah, Tim. *The Serbs: History, Myth and the Destruction of Yugoslavia*. New Haven, CT & London: Yale University Press, 1997.

Rohde, David. *A Safe Area – Srebrenica: Europe's Worst Massacre Since the Second World War*. London: Pocket Books, 1997.

Rushdie, Salman (2002). "Step Across This Line" (The Tanner Lectures on Human Values, Yale University, 2002). In: *Step Across This Line: Collected Non-Fiction, 1992-2002*. London: Vintage, 2003, p. 407-42.

Shakespeare, William. *The Tempest*. In: *The Complete Works*. Ed. Peter Alexander. London & Glasgow: Collins, 1951, p. 1-26.

Shattuck, John. *Freedom on Fire: Human Rights Wars and America's Response*. Cambridge, MA & London: Harvard University Press, 2003.

Shawcross, William (2000). *Deliver Us From Evil: Warlords and Peacekeepers in a World of Endless Conflict*. London: Bloomsbury, 2001.

Steyn, Mark. "Nouveau Warfare: Clinton Administration's Involvement with the Strike Against Yugoslavia." In: *National Review*, May 3, 1999. Web page, <http://www.findarticles.com/p/articles/mi_m1282/is_8_51/a i_54391010> (Accessed 30.11.2004)

West, Rebecca. *Black Lamb and Grey Falcon: A Journey through Yugoslavia*. New York: Viking, 1941.

INDEX

"Antony" (Plutarch), 187
Antony and Cleopatra (Shakespeare), 159, 166-167, 174, 187
Aphrodite (Louÿs), 167-169, 186
Apollonius of Rhodes, 165
An Area of Darkness (Naipaul), 172, 186
Aristainetus, 168, 185
Aristarchus, 163
Aristophanes (the scholar, not the playwright), 163
Arouet, François-Marie—SEE: Voltaire
Around the World in 80 Days (film), 110, 121—SEE ALSO: *Le Tour de monde en quatre-vingt jours*
Art and Illusion: A Study in the Psychology of Pictorial Representation (Gombrich), 39, 52
Arthashastra (Kautilya), 102, 118
Ashes of Immortality: Widow-Burning in India—SEE: *Cendres d'immortalité*
Asia (magazine), 53
Asia in the Making of Europe. Volume I: The Century of Discovery (Lach), 119
"At the End of the Passage" (Kipling), 85
Atharva-Veda, 102
Atlantic (website), 92
Austen, Jane, 123, 133, 137-138
Austen-Leigh, James Edward, 138
Aziyadé (Loti), 17, 33
Bai, Kuttu, 101
Baker, James, 193
Baker, Judith, 27, 31
Baker, W. Howard ("Bill Rekab"), 44, 51
Baldick, Robert, 186
Ballard, J. G., 5-6, 57-68
"Ballard's Worlds" (Amis), 68
Balthazar (Durrell), 177-185
Bamboo Hell (Finlay), 44, 52
"Bangkok—the New Vienna" (Weeks), 156
Barczaitis, Rainer, 45
Barger, Florence, 172
Barrie, J. M., 57, 68
BBC News (website), 117-118
BBC radio, 182
The Beach: The History of Paradise on Earth (Lencek & Bosker), 155
Beauchamp, Henry K., 117-118
Bell, Clara, 33
Beneke, Jürgen, 5, 139, 154
Benner, Allen Rogers, 184
Bennett, William, 146
Bentinck, William, Lord, 100
Bevan, F. L., 142, 148, 154

209

Erotic Letters of Aristainetus—SEE: *Erotische Briefe*
Erotische Briefe (Aristainetos), 168
The Ethnic Detective: Chester Hines, Harry Kemelman, Tony Hillerman (Freese), 81
Euripides, 164
Ewer, Walter, 116
"Exotisch wie die Deutschen" ("E.D.B."), 51
The Faber Book of Epigrams and Epitaphs (ed. Grigson), 185
The Far Pavilions (novel, Kaye; TV version, dir. Duffell), 111, 119, 121
Fedden, Robin, 170
Fedrici, Cesare de, 104
Felsenstein, Frank, 156
"Female Infanticide: Old Reasons, New Techniques" (Venkatesan), 120
Fielding, Xan, 33
"Fifteenth Idyll" (Theocritus), 165-166
Figueira, Dorothy, 104, 118
"Film Highlight's [*sic*] Widows' Plight" (Anand), 117
Finlay, Bernard, 44, 52
Flacelière, Robert, 168-169, 185
"Die Flambierte Frau: Sate in European Culture" (Figueria), 118
Flaubert, Gustave, 16, 48, 52, 161, 185
Flaubert in Egypt: A Sensibility on Tour: A Narrative Drawn from Gustave Flaubert's Travel Notes & Letters (ed. & tr. Steegmuller), 52, 185
Flaws in the Glass: A Self-Portrait (White), 187
Fleming, Ian, 49, 76, 81
Flindt, Rosalind, 6
Foote, Paul, 33
Forbes, Francis H., 184
Ford, Harrison, 49
Fordyce, C. J., 164, 185
Forster, E. M., 14, 28, 32, 147-148, 155, 159, 165, 169, 171-175, 185-186
Foucault, Michel, 38
Fowles, John, 159, 186
"Frankfurter Polizeivize angeklagt" (anon.), 92
Fraser, G. S., 177, 182, 186
Freedom on Fire: Human Rights Wars and America's Response (Shattuck), 204
Freese, Peter, 69-70, 81
French, Philip, 60, 66, 68
"From the Deserts of Belgium to the Jungles of Korea" (Jarman), 5, 37-56
"Fueling the Fire of the Sati Debate" (Pinney), 119
Furbank, P. N., 173, 186
Fussell, Paul, 150-151, 155
Galtung, Johan, 69, 81
Gandhi, Indira, 127-128, 131-132

Griffith, R., 120
Grigson, Geoffrey, 185
Grindlay, Captain, 108-109
Grossberg, Lawrence, 120
Gruesser, John Cullen, 38, 52
Grundlagen zur Literatur in englischer Sprache—Indien (ed. Stilz), 53
Guardian Unlimited (website0, 138
Guest, Val, 31
Haag, Michael, 171, 185
Hadrian, 145
Haggard, Sir Henry Rider, 9, 32
Haig, T. W., 117
Hammerstein, Oscar, 42
Hampden-Turner, Charles, 90, 93
Hannoversche Allgemeine Zeitung (magazine), 51
Harlow, Barbara, 107, 118
Harrison, Rex, 42
Harsha, 103
Hawley, John Stratton, 101, 118-119
Heat and Dust (Jhabvala), 28
Die Heitherethei und ihr Widerspiel (Ludwig), 46
"Henry Miller" (Durrell; Miller), 185
"Heraclitus" (Callimachus), 185
Heraclitus of Halicarnassus, 165, 185
Herder, Johann Gottfried von, 104
A Hero of Our Time—SEE: Geroy nashego vremeni
The Hidden Flower (Buck), 18, 31
Hiebel, Henriette—SEE: La Jana
High Noon (film; dir. Zinnemann), 90, 93
Hildesheim University, 6
Hill, George Birkbeck, 154-155
Hillen, Ernest (Ernst), 65, 68
Hillerman, Tony, 70, 81
The Hindu (website), 120
Hindu Art (Blurton), 117
Hindu Literary Review (website), 117
*Hindu Manners, Customs and Ceremonies—SEE: Moeurs, institutions et
    cérémonies des peuples de l'Inde*
Hinduism Today (website), 119
Hines, Chester, 81
Hislop, Richard, 27, 32
The Histories (Tacitus), 187
"The History of Albrecht Dürer's Rhinoceros in Zoological Literature"
    (Cole), 51
A History of India (Thapar), 120
Hitler's Willing Executioners: Ordinary Germans and the Holocaust
    (Goldhagen), 38, 52
Hitrec, Joseph, 203

James Bond (series; Fleming), 49, 76
Japan (MacFarlane; in Yokoyama), 48, 53
Japan—SEE: *Madame Chrysanthème*
*Japan in the Victorian Mind: A Study of Stereotyped Images of a Nation,
     1850-80* (Yokoyama), 53
The Japanese Corpse (Wetering), 74-81
A Japanese Mirror: Heroes and Villains of Japanese Culture (Buruma),
     80
The Japanese Tradition in British and American Literature (Miner), 33
Japan's Orient: Rendering Pasts into History (Tanaka), 53
Jarman, Francis, 11, 25, 32, 38, 42, 52, 105, 118, 147, 152, 154-155,
     194-203
Jarvis, C. S., Major—SEE: "Rameses"
The Jewel in the Crown (Scott), 14-16, 34
"J.G. Ballard: Through the Eyes of a Child" (Jarman), 5-6, 57-68
Jhabvala, Cyrus, 28, 32
Jhabvala, Ruth Prawer, 28-31
Johnson, Paul, 142, 155
Johnson, Samuel, 146, 149, 154-155
Jordan, Neil, 35
Joseph (Indian Christian priest), 104
Journal of American Culture, 156
Judah, Tim, 192, 203
Justine (Durrell), 176-185
Juvenal, 166, 186
Kämmer, Gerhard-Dieter, 33
Kanwar, Om, 114-115
Kanwar, Roop, 101, 114-116, 119
Karadžić, Radovan, 193
Karmakar, Rahul, 100, 118
"Kahmir Bans the Widow Word" (Hussain), 118
De Kat van Brigadier de Gier (Wetering), 75-76, 81
Die Katze von Brigadier de Gier: Kriminalstories—SEE: *De Kat van
     Brigadier de Gier*
Kaul, H. K., 107-108, 118
Kautilya, 102, 118
Kavafis, Konstantinos—SEE: Cavafy, Constantine
Kaye, M. M., 92, 111, 119
Keating, H. R. F., 69-70, 81
Keith, Agnes Newton, 60-61, 68
Kelsey Museum Newsletter (website), 186
Kemelman, Harry, 70, 81
Kerr, Deborah, 42
Khilji, Ala-ud-din, Sultan of Delhi, 98
Khushwant Singh, 123-138
Khushwant Singh's Big Book of Malice (Singh), 129, 138
Kimono for a Corpse (Melville), 81
The Kindness of Women (Ballard), 57-68

Said, Edward W., 11, 34, 38, 52
"Salome Theatre of Dreams"—SEE: Traumtheater Salome
Sämtliche Werke nach Epochen seines Schreibens (ed. Wild), 118
Sartorius, Joachim, 161, 179-180, 187
The Satanic Verses (Rushdie), 125, 138
Satapatha Brahmana (ancient text), 111-112
"Sati"—SEE: "Burning Women"
"Sati as Profit Versus Sati as a Spectacle: The Public Debate on Roop
    Kanwar's Death" (Nandy), 119
Sati, the Blessing and the Curse: The Burning of Wives in India (ed.
    Hawley), 118
Sati: Widow Burning in India (Narasimhan), 119
Sattin, Anthony, 161-162, 171, 187
Savill, Mervyn, 32
Schneider, Wolfgang Christian, 45
Scindia, Daulat Rao, Prince of Gwalior, 108-109
Scott, Paul, 14-16, 27-28, 34
Scott, Walter, Sir, 189
Scott-Kilvert, Ian, 156
Selected Letters of E. M. Forster, Volume One, 1879-1920 (Forster), 171-
    172, 186
Seleucus Nicator, 98
Selwyn Lloyd (Thorpe), 156
Sen, Mala, 112-114, 120
"Seoul Brothers" (O'Rourke), 143, 156
The Serbs: History, Myth and the Destruction of Yugoslavia (Judah),
    203
The Sergeant's Cat and Other Stories—SEE: *De Kat van Brigadier de
    Gier*
Seth, Vikram, 123-138
Sex and Society in Graeco-Roman Egypt (Montserrat), 186
Sex, Scotch and Scholarship: Selected Writings (Singh), 129, 138
Shakespeare, William, 159, 166-167, 174, 187, 204
Shankaracharya of Puri, 101-102
Shattuck, John, 189-190, 193, 204
Shawcross, William, 190, 192-193, 204
The Sheik (film), 27
Shelden, Michael, 21, 34
Siamese Harem Life—SEE: *The Romance of the Harem*
Singer, Charles, 51
The Sixteen Satires (Juvenal), 186
"Sixth Satire" (Juvenal), 166
Slaves of the Gods (Mayo), 105, 119
"SMEs and Intercultural Communication" (Jarman), 155
Smith, Malcolm, 40, 42, 52
Smollett, Tobias, 143, 153, 156
Social Science Information (journal), 81
The Social System (Parsons), 93

www.ingramcontent.com/pod-product-compliance
Lightning Source LLC
Chambersburg PA
CBHW022017090426
42739CB00006BA/172

* 9 780809 511884 *